P9-DUQ-456

studies in jazz

Institute of Jazz Studies
Rutgers—The State University of New Jersey
General Editors: Dan Morgenstern and Edward Berger

1. BENNY CARTER: A Life in American Music, *by Morroe Berger, Edward Berger, and James Patrick, 2 vols., 1982*
2. ART TATUM: A Guide to His Recorded Music, *by Arnold Laubich and Ray Spencer, 1982*
3. ERROLL GARNER: The Most Happy Piano, *by James M. Doran, 1995*
4. JAMES P. JOHNSON: A Case of Mistaken Identity, *by Scott E. Brown;* Discography 1917–1950, *by Robert Hilbert, 1986*
5. PEE WEE ERWIN: This Horn for Hire, *as told to Warren W. Vaché Sr., 1987*
6. BENNY GOODMAN: Listen to His Legacy, *by D. Russell Connor, 1988*
7. ELLINGTONIA: The Recorded Music of Duke Ellington and His Sidemen, *by W. E. Timner, 1988; 4th ed., 1996*
8. THE GLENN MILLER ARMY AIR FORCE BAND: Sustineo Alas / I Sustain the Wings, *by Edward F. Polic;* Foreword *by George T. Simon, 1989*
9. SWING LEGACY, *by Chip Deffaa, 1989*
10. REMINISCING IN TEMPO: The Life and Times of a Jazz Hustler, *by Teddy Reig, with Edward Berger, 1990*
11. IN THE MAINSTREAM: 18 Portraits in Jazz, *by Chip Deffaa, 1992*
12. BUDDY DeFRANCO: A Biographical Portrait and Discography, *by John Kuehn and Arne Astrup, 1993*
13. PEE WEE SPEAKS: A Discography of Pee Wee Russell, *by Robert Hilbert, with David Niven, 1992*
14. SYLVESTER AHOLA: The Gloucester Gabriel, *by Dick Hill, 1993*
15. THE POLICE CARD DISCORD, *by Maxwell T. Cohen, 1993*
16. TRADITIONALISTS AND REVIVALISTS IN JAZZ, *by Chip Deffaa, 1993*
17. BASSICALLY SPEAKING: An Oral History of George Duvivier, *by Edward Berger;* Musical Analysis *by David Chevan, 1993*
18. TRAM: The Frank Trumbauer Story, *by Philip R. Evans and Larry F. Kiner, with William Trumbauer, 1994*

19. TOMMY DORSEY: On the Side, *by Robert L. Stockdale, 1995*
20. JOHN COLTRANE: A Discography and Musical Biography, *by Yasuhiro Fujioka, with Lewis Porter and Yoh-ichi Hamada, 1995*
21. RED HEAD: A Chronological Survey of "Red" Nichols and His Five Pennies, *by Stephen M. Stroff, 1996*
22. THE RED NICHOLS STORY: After Intermission 1942–1965, *by Philip R. Evans, Stanley Hester, Stephen Hester, and Linda Evans, 1997*
23. BENNY GOODMAN: Wrappin' It Up, *by D. Russell Connor, 1996*
24. CHARLIE PARKER AND THEMATIC IMPROVISATION, *by Henry Martin, 1996*
25. BACK BEATS AND RIM SHOTS: The Johnny Blowers Story, *by Warren W. Vaché Sr., 1997*
26. DUKE ELLINGTON: A Listener's Guide, *by Eddie Lambert, 1998*
27. SERGE CHALOFF: A Musical Biography and Discography, *by Vladimir Simosko, 1998*
28. HOT JAZZ: From Harlem to Storyville, *by David Griffiths, 1998*
29. ARTIE SHAW: A Musical Biography and Discography, *by Vladimir Simosko, 2000*
30. JIMMY DORSEY: A Study in Contrasts, *by Robert L. Stockdale, 1998*
31. STRIDE!: Fats, Jimmy, Lion, Lamb and All the Other Ticklers, *by John L. Fell and Terkild Vinding, 1999*
32. GIANT STRIDES: The Legacy of Dick Wellstood, *by Edward N. Meyer, 1999*
33. JAZZ GENTRY: Aristocrats of the Music World, *by Warren W. Vaché Sr., 1999*
34. THE UNSUNG SONGWRITERS: America's Masters of Melody, *by Warren W. Vaché Sr., 2000*
35. THE MUSICAL WORLD OF J. J. JOHNSON, *by Joshua Berrett and Louis G. Bourgois III, 1999*
36. THE LADIES WHO SING WITH THE BAND, *by Betty Bennett, 2000*
37. AN UNSUNG CAT: The Life and Music of Warne Marsh, *by Safford Chamberlain, 2000*

The Ladies Who Sing with the Band

Betty Bennett

Studies in Jazz

The Scarecrow Press, Inc.
Lanham, Maryland, and London
2000

SCARECROW PRESS, INC.

Published in the United States of America
by Scarecrow Press, Inc.
4720 Boston Way, Lanham, Maryland 20706
http://www.scarecrowpress.com

4 Pleydell Gardens, Folkestone
Kent CT20 2DN, England

British Library Cataloguing in Publication Information Available

Library of Congress Cataloging-in-Publication Data

Bennett, Betty, 1921–
The ladies who sing with the band / Betty Bennett.
p. cm. (Studies in jazz; no. 36)
Includes index.
ISBN 0-8108-3714-5
1. Bennett, Betty, 1921– . 2. Singers—United States—Biography.
I. Title. II. Series.
ML420.B34375 A3 2000
782.42165'092—dc21
[B] 99-049460

∞™ The paper used in this publication meets the minimum requirements of American National Standard for Information Sciences—Permanence of Paper for Printed Library Materials, ANSI/NISO Z39.48–1992.
Manufactured in the United States of America.

This book is lovingly dedicated to my mother, Doris Wortman Bennett.
Anything I may have accomplished I owe to her.

Contents

Acknowledgments

My daughters, Claudia Previn and Alicia Previn Lynch, and my dear husband, Mundell Lowe.

Editor's Foreword

Betty Lowe's book represents a valuable addition to the literature of jazz on several levels. It is an entertaining and unpretentious chronicle of a life in American popular music, recounted with wit and honesty. But it is more than the story of one talented artist, however interesting that might be. The author evokes a bygone era when "territory" and "name" bands—each with its own "girl singer"—crisscrossed the country. For those who grew up during this musically exciting and turbulent time, Bennett's account will bring back many memories. For those who never experienced it, she provides a fascinating insight into a unique period in American cultural history when art and commerce merged to produce a popular music of extraordinarily high quality.

The author's career intersected with many of the icons of jazz and popular music, among them Nat King Cole, Dizzy Gillespie, Georgie Auld, Claude Thornhill, Charlie Ventura, Benny Goodman, and Charlie Barnet. The many anecdotes about these personalities enlighten and entertain, as does her entirely unselfconscious discussion of her marriage to André Previn and her relationship with her husband, guitar great Mundell Lowe. Along the way, Lowe offers many insights into the mechanics of singing as well as the complex interplay between singer and accompanists.

Finally, the book deals with several issues that transcend music. The entertainment industry—particularly the jazz world—was an early area of black-white professional and personal interaction. Moreover, the traveling big band represented a unique instance of women in an all-male workplace. Bennett confronts these issues of race and gender in a refreshingly forthright manner.

—Edward Berger

Foreword

Girl singers in every big band were an integral part of the whole and a big draw. In the beginning their role was secondary, and they didn't even get to sing the first chorus of a song. Later, the emphasis changed, and the singer became a star.

My own music career really started to flourish near the end of the big band era. In those memorable days in the 1940s, I worked with many girl singers on their way up. Betty Bennett was one of those who stood out for her way with everything from romantic ballads to up-tempo swing. She sang a tune her way, and she sang it very well.

By 1943 I was living in Los Angeles at 1107 Arapahoe Street, rooming with a houseful of musicians. I was usually to be found practicing in my room on the second floor. A drummer who also lived there came up the stairs one day with Betty Bennett in tow and introduced us. Almost immediately she started singing along while I continued to play the guitar.

Soon afterwards, I went one night to a place on Eighth Street where Nat Cole's Trio was playing and saw her again. About two or three months later I had a gig every Tuesday night in a legendary little Hollywood club called the Suzie Q where Erroll Garner and Jack Teagarden often played. I called Betty and asked her to come sing for me; she did for several weeks. Later, when I was in New York with Artie Shaw's band and she was a Wave in the Navy, I saw her again. I recorded with her a few years after that with André Previn and Shorty Rogers on her *Nobody Else But Me* album and by then she was singing like a star. Then through the years we were on separate coasts. I was playing in Europe a lot and lost track of her.

We both eventually moved to San Diego about the same time and enjoy our friendship again. Betty recently gave me a copy of her

1990 recording *The Song Is You* and I wasn't mistaken in my admiration. She sounds better than ever. For me, she's one of the best. In this book, she's writing about something she has truly lived and loved.

—Barney Kessel

Introduction

Some of the most wonderful years of my life were spent traveling on a bus with seventeen men. It was hard, exhausting, and often frustrating. The "girl singer" had a unique role to play. Given little respect by much of the band, she sits on the bandstand, singing only occasionally. The rest of the time she must look as if she is having the time of her life. This includes grinning, clapping, bouncing, anything to belie the fact that she probably hasn't had enough sleep, and has had to put on her makeup and gown in the ballroom ladies' room surrounded by a gaggle of women who seem to be fascinated by her every move. Why is it then that I enjoyed every backbreaking minute of it?

There have been a couple of books written "as told to" by girl singers, but as far as I know, mine is the only one written by the girl singer herself.

I am married to my fourth husband, and to avoid confusion when I mention one out of the blue, here are their names: number one, Robert Coleman Shevak, nicknamed "Iggy" after a comic strip; number two, André Previn; number three, Les Lampson; number four, Mundell Lowe. After twenty-four years of marriage to Mundell, I think I can safely say, "I finally got it right!" It seems to be a tradition of the girl singer to marry a pianist, but I married a rhythm section! Iggy, my first, was a bass player; André, my second, a pianist; number three was an aberration, a television booth announcer; then Mundell, a guitar player.

The preponderance of girl singers married to pianists is remarkable. Most of the rest are married to other musicians, managers, or arrangers. The lifestyle is very hard on relationships, so the fact that the music gives couples so much in common can only enhance the attraction. (Besides, if you're traveling constantly, it is difficult to sustain a relationship with the boy back home or wherever he may be.) On the bandstand, however, the daily contact, shared hardships, and hilarity can bring couples together and help cement their relationship. (Propinquity helps.)

If there are terms in this book that are unfamiliar, I apologize, but I have made them as simple as I possibly can. Any failure to understand is clearly the result of my inability and not that of the reader.

Chronology

BETTY BENNETT:
Born Lincoln, Nebraska, October 23, 1921
First territory band job, Royce Stoenner, 1940
Famous Door, New York, 1941
Milt Page Quartet, New York and Atlantic City, 1942
Georgie Auld band, 1943
Mistress of Ceremonies and singer on CBS coast to coast when in Navy, 1945–46. Show called "Service Time"; its purpose was recruitment and entertainment
Claude Thornhill band, 1946
Alvino Rey's band, 1947–49
Stan Kenton All-Stars, 1949
Charlie Ventura, 1949–50
Woody Herman's small band, 1950
Worked as single in Facks, Blackhawk, Hungry i in San Francisco, 1951
Charlie Barnet's band, 1952
Married André Previn, 1952. Three albums: Atlantic, Trend, United Artists with André Previn
Benny Goodman's band, 1957
Mister Kelly's in Chicago, Shelly's Manne Hole, Dino's, Ye Little Club, Los Angeles, 1957–62
Ronnie Scott's Jazz Club, London, off and on, 1963–66. Television and radio shows abroad
Back in Los Angeles: The Times, Donte's, Carmelo's, Le Café, and Alfonse's
Munster Jazz Festival, Munster, France
London, Pizza on the Park and Pizza Express
San Diego, Palace Bar, Horton Grande Hotel, appearances at Jazz Societies
New CD from Fresh Sound Records: "I Thought About You"

• 1 •

The Early Years

In the late '30s when I was in high school in Hamburg, Iowa, I used to listen to Claude Thornhill's band on my small radio very late at night, fantasizing about singing with that great band. Ten years later my fantasy was fulfilled, though it turned out to be more torment than fulfillment!

Being a girl singer on the road with a band is a strange and fascinating way of life. You're the only female traveling with seventeen men. When you are constantly on the road, it is almost impossible to develop a meaningful or lasting relationship with a gentleman caller, or maintain a friendship with a close girlfriend, for that matter.

I spent the first fifteen years of my singing life traveling on the road with bands. First, territory bands—these were bands that performed in specific parts of the country. The first band I worked in toured the Midwest, where I was born and raised. My mother was a thwarted classical pianist who played jazz at night in a band her brother formed. Although her name was Doris, she was nicknamed "Dot," and when she would take an improvisatory chorus or two, the band would shout, "Get hot, Dot!" My uncle had this phrase painted on his banjo case, and I have mourned ever since that the case fell apart before I could preserve it.

My mother is totally responsible for my interest in jazz. From my childhood I heard Count Basie, Duke Ellington, and Fats Waller, a few of her favorites. I spent many a night in my childhood sitting beside the piano while my mother played her various gigs. Occasionally I was coaxed into singing some simple pop tune.

Although I was born in Lincoln, Nebraska, at age four I moved with my family to Hamburg, Iowa, where my father was hired as a baker at Pinkie's, a restaurant/bakery. My father reminded me of his most embarrassing moment, brought on by seven-year-old me. Due to terminal whimsy, I don't always hear things the way people say them. I either take a different meaning of a word or pronounce it the way it is spelled. This tendency was a great help in learning to spell, but in this case it backfired. While strolling through the bakery one day, I asked my father if I could have a "dog nut." Even I realized that something was really wrong because the three bakers fell silent. Finally my father gave me a "doughnut" and I left. Of course, it was years before I put that together!

In grade school there were several children who were needy, so every morning at 10 a.m. they were given milk to drink. I was a scrawny child and was humiliated daily because they also made me drink the milk. That may have been the day a snob was born!

Ever since childhood I have had a horror of being late. In kindergarten the few times I started to school and realized I'd be late, I slunk back home. This led to a funny scene one day. When I got home, my mother wasn't there, so I decided to make myself some breakfast. We must have had the first electric stove ever invented, and my mother had taught me how to use it. I fixed an egg and some toast, and when my mother returned and saw me calmly sitting at the table eating my food, she was both flabbergasted and proud.

Someone had recommended my mother as the perfect person to write music for a set of lyrics written by a man from an adjoining town. The lyrics were indescribably awful. I still remember the title: "This is why we like to go to Washington." Mercifully, I can remember nothing more. My mother felt guilty accepting the man's money, but I did not. He paid me fifty cents each time I sang it for him.

Around the house my mother played her Duke Ellington, Count Basie, and Fats Waller records. Years later, when Basie was playing a nightclub in Los Angeles, my husband and I took her to hear the band. One of the local musicians came over, met my mother, and said, "It must be quite a thrill for you to hear Count Basie, Mrs. Bennett. Is this the first time?" "No," my mother replied, "I used to hear him back in Kansas City." Mel Lewis, the drummer, was there that night and came up to complain that the band was dragging. Irv Cotler, also a drummer, said, "Nonsense, they're just settling." It made sense to me!

I think my mother's very favorite band was Ellington's. She read that he was playing at the Playmor Ballroom in St. Joseph, Missouri. For my sixteenth birthday she paid for a twenty-three-year-old friend of mine and me to take the train to St. Joseph to hear the Ellington band. The ballroom was hung with silver leaves which covered the entire ceiling. I was amazed that the band didn't use stands. It was a unique sight to see the musicians sitting on the chairs with nothing in front of them. And the band! Rex Stewart, Ray Nance, Ben Webster, Johnny Hodges, to name only a few of the legends. Ivie Anderson was the girl singer. An electrifying night.

I have always had an excellent sense of time or rhythm and through the years have had piano players attempt to make me lose my place by playing intricate patterns and sometimes changing keys several times during a song. I thrived on this. They never threw me. I attribute this (not particularly astounding) facility to colic. As a baby, I had such severe colic that my parents took turns walking me all night, playing the Victrola and singing to me as they paced. At about six months they noticed that I was bobbing my head in time to one of the records. Disbelieving, they changed records, and I altered my bobbing accordingly.

In Hamburg, my mother played local club dates, but for fourteen years her principal job was playing piano for the silent movie theater. What a bonanza for me to have free admission to all the new movies! Actually, I was allowed to attend only on the weekend. Only cowboy movies were shown then, which (I suddenly realize) may be why I always have had an aversion to Westerns. During the week my mother played solo, but over the weekend the theater owner augmented the "band," and her best friend, a violinist, would join her. One evening they were playing a ballad, and my mother was dismayed to find that she couldn't remember the bridge. Confident that her violinist friend, Ruth, would remember it, she played gamely on. The trouble was that Ruth couldn't remember the bridge either and was equally confident that my mother would come through. That was one long ballad!

Today when musicians can't remember the bridge, they shout "Sears and Roebuck," which is a simple harmonic bridge as heard in the song "Honeysuckle Rose," until they get through the memory lapse or to the last eight bars—whichever comes first.

My first grade teacher in elementary school was a single woman who was dating the principal. I made the mistake of teasing her about her romance. She so resented this that, in that very important year when you learn to add, she completely ignored me, with the result that I either use dot-dot-dot, depending on the number being added, or failing that, I use my fingers. I must confess that I have finally trained myself to add, and although I now use a calculator, occasionally I use the old-fashioned way to see if I can still do it.

Another problem I had was learning the multiplication tables. My mother solved this in an unusual way. She would play a chord on the piano and I would intone, "Two times two is four." A new chord. "Two times three is six." Another chord . . . you get the idea. All the way through the twelvsies. (No, I don't have to have chords to be able to multiply.)

My father had something of a drinking problem. Although I didn't realize it at the time, mother must have given him an ultimatum, because suddenly, just as I was to enter the third grade, my mother and I moved to Omaha, Nebraska, ostensibly to take care of her brothers. She had three, all of whom worked at the *Omaha World Herald* as linotype operators. What a thrill it was to visit them at work at night.

Before mother registered me for the third grade in school, she had me memorize my home address. I was really kind of a hick, so this turned out to be important. I can still remember the address: 2630 Davenport. (My present address takes a little more thought!) The school took up an entire block, and when I came out in the afternoon, I left by a different door, totally negating my directions. After wandering about for a half hour or so, a nice young man came up and asked if I was okay. I told him of my plight and the dear chap walked me home. Can you imagine how dangerous that would be today?

My mother's sister was married to a man who owned a little club on the outskirts of Omaha. Mother played piano in the club on the weekend. On the piano was the obligatory "kitty"—tips for the piano player. One night a gent came up to her and asked her to sing some song. She explained that she wasn't a singer, whereupon he slipped a twenty dollar bill into the kitty. Mother said, "What would you like me to sing?"

My third grade teacher in Omaha was every child's nightmare. I had a tremendous underbite, and very few days passed in which she didn't call me up in front of the class to show off my bridgework. I was heartbroken and cried a lot. We didn't stay in Omaha very long, but before we left, the teacher called my mother in and told her that I was so nervous she was sure I'd be in an insane asylum before I was twelve. My mother didn't realize that she could have reported this frightful woman and always felt that she'd somehow let me down. We were grateful to go back to Hamburg and to be reunited with my father.

Back at school in Hamburg the seventh and eighth grades were in the same room, divided by a large aisle. In my eighth grade year the school decided to choose a king and queen from the eighth grade and present them in a festive evening in the high school gym. To this end, we were all given ballots. Richard Mansfield won "king" and I won "queen." I was thrilled until the girls in the eighth grade who had their own ideas about who the queen should be demanded a new ballot. I still won. This was the first of two major blows delivered to me in Hamburg's school system, and with my already sagging self-confidence I took a long time to recover. My aunt from Omaha lent me a perfectly beautiful rose taffeta long ruffled dress to wear. I was in the girl's room putting it on behind a shower curtain (as my classmates well knew) when I heard them saying what an ugly dress, etc. That kind of gratuitous cruelty has haunted me through the years, and I have tried to keep it out of my own behavior.

After Pinkie's bakery closed, my father opened his own bakery which he, a couple of bakers, and my mother operated. I waited on customers before and after school but without enthusiasm because each morning when I arrived at school the other students would take long deep sniffs of my hair and say, "You smell like doughnuts." I hated it.

In the bakery, the façade of a house with a door on the left side and a "window" in the middle was built to separate the work area from the display cases in front. Baked goods could be passed through this window. In back of the window was a room where bread was sliced, pies assembled, and food prepared for our family to eat. Behind that second room was the actual bakery, the oven, counter space, supplies and everything that was required to put out the day's goods. In order to spare the people working in the back, my mother gave herself, my father, one of his bakers, and me a number. If you were coming into the bakery, you simply called out your number, and the workers immediately knew who it was and stayed where they were. My number was "three." (I wouldn't say Hamburg was small, but our telephone number was thirteen!)

Every day my father would set out with his bread and rolls and pies, delivering to the grocery stores and restaurants. He whistled incessantly, a distinctive whistle that had a very wide vibrato. It was quite funny. One day, as he appeared, whistling some tune, my mother began to sing another tune. Next time he came in, sure enough, he was whistling the tune my mother sang. This became a game my father never caught on to. One day Mother sang "Nola." To the uninitiated, a very fast song. We broke up when Dad came in at least trying to whistle it.

We always hired a high school girl to help in the bakery. This one was extremely shy. We had a small mixer for cakes and such, and one of the blades needed washing. Mother and I heard my father ask this poor girl "if she'd washed his kadingbob yet." This may have gone unnoticed if mother and I hadn't screamed with laughter. My father had no idea why we were laughing.

My father had a great sense of humor and he needed it, being around mother and me. We always had a cat around the bakery as the buildings were very old and we were in a constant battle against mice. My father always named the cats. One day at lunch our latest mouse fiend, named Oz, strolled by. There followed an inadvertent old-fashioned minstrel show. I asked my father why he called the cat "Oz." (There was a sports columnist out of Chicago called Oz Black unbeknownst to mother and me.) Dad said, "Don't you know Oz Black?" I replied, "You is?" He turned to my mother with a look of helplessness. That was my first joke. I apologize to the NAACP.

I shall never forget the sheer terror of moving from elementary school to high school. It didn't help matters that our math teacher, Mr. Hansen (whom we called "Teddy Bear Hansen") took an instant dislike to me. I cannot be called a poor math student; I am a completely hopeless one, and he obviously knew that, which may account for his hostility. Everything that could go wrong seemed to happen in his class or in study hall when he was the monitor. I confess I was always seated in the front in his class because I was sassy and noisy. One of my classmates put a thumbtack in my seat one day before algebra class. It backfired because I didn't even know it until he told me. When he left the room for a second, I put the tack in his seat. Talk about overreacting! He made such a fuss that Mr. Hansen sent me to the principal's office. It was not the first time.

Study hall was a large room, seating perhaps seventy-five students. Each row had two attached seats, then an aisle and another two seats, going all the way from the front of the room to the back. It was here that my worst Hansen nightmares took place. I have always loved "red hots," those small red cinnamon drops, and every day I'd take a handful from the bakery candy case to school. So they wouldn't make noise, I took them out of the bag and put them on my lap. I raised my hand for permission to go to the girl's room, forgetting the red hots, and they all fell on the floor, making a tremendous racket. Off I went to the principal's office.

Another day in study hall we all heard a car horn blasting outside the window. I remarked to my seatmate, "What idiot would come to school and expect the right person to recognize the horn and come to the window?!" You guessed it. It was *my* idiot! Some swain from an adjoining town had decided to look me up! I didn't go to the principal's office that day, but when someone actually came to fetch me for my idiot friend, I was thoroughly humiliated. Of course it happened on Hansen's watch!

I learned that the high school orchestra was looking for a cymbal player, so I tried out and got the job. Hamburg also had a marching band and someone was needed to play bass drum. My good time sense got me that job. It was my task to "dress up the line," meaning to see to it that the line was straight. We played for all the football games and would do our "routines" at the half.

The band was asked to march in a huge parade in Des Moines, Iowa, underwritten by the local Des Moines newspaper. It was bitter cold, and the poor brass players were barely able to get their lips off their mouthpieces, much less play! After the parade several of us decided to go to the movies. *Ecstasy* was playing in an art theater, and although we were only fifteen and the legal age to see the movie was eighteen, somehow they let us in. I had no idea I would be so embarrassed. We were all embarrassed, girls *and* boys! The symbolism of the bee and flower was lost on us! What an innocent time.

The science teacher and football coach was Andy Selk. I adored him. He taught science, which was my first period. He also brought me up short when I decided to change the spelling of "Betty" to "Bette." (Bette was a fellow classmate who became a dear friend.) When we handed in our papers, they were folded in half lengthwise with our names on the outside. The day after my name change Mr. Selk was quizzing us. He called on me. However, he pronounced my newly spelled Bette like "Bet-teh." I got the message and have been Betty ever since.

The second semester the schedule changed so that band practice was moved to first period. The powers that be said I'd have to take a later and different class as I was needed in band practice. I was so crushed I said I'd quit the band. It turned out to be a case of inadvertent blackmail! They needed me for the band, so they let me take any class I wanted as long as it wasn't in first period.

I loved school and looked forward to it every day. It was an extremely busy time for me because I had orchestra practice, marching band practice, mixed chorus, and girls' chorus and I appeared in every play staged while I was in high school. There were also the weekly piano and voice lessons with the obligatory practicing. Although I was only five foot six, I played guard on the women's basketball team. I was fouled a lot but happily I was a demon free-thrower so I didn't mind.

By this time the theater owner had converted to talkies, so my movie freeloading days were over. My mother was now working in the bakery days, playing for the Kiwanis club meetings and the occasional dance job at night. She played organ at the Baptist church and directed the choir. (She was chagrined when, in her first year as choir director, two of the choir members became pregnant and had to get married.) I sang soprano in the choir and an occasional solo on Sunday. Also on Sunday the movie attraction changed from cowboy movies to musicals. I was never allowed to go to the movies on Sunday unless I had gone to church that morning.

My grandmother gave me a pair of what I think were called "Cuban heels." They were white leather and mesh. (I wouldn't be caught dead in them today!) I had a date for the movies and decided to wear my new shoes. The trouble was that they were at least a size too small! I removed them immediately in the movie theater, but when we got up to leave, my feet had swollen to such an extent that it was impossible for me to get my shoes on. My date had to go to my house to get a pair of shoes that fit me. I was mortified.

Although the high school boys my age had not learned to dance as yet, we girls became fanatics, dancing to the jukebox in a local restaurant every afternoon after school. One Sunday the new minister at the Baptist church delivered a stern lecture on the evils of dancing. I decided to seek a new denomination and went through the Christian, Methodist, and Presbyterian churches, trying to find a church that condoned dancing. At that time, none of the churches permitted dancing, so I stopped going to church. I can't believe that my goal was to marry a good dancer who made ten thousand dollars a year! I have been married four times and all my husbands were atrocious dancers, but happily, all made much more than ten thousand a year. Speaking of dancing, during my marriage to André

Previn, he was assigned to write a score to a musical starring Fred Astaire. One day André visited the set, and after watching the incredibly gifted Astaire go through his routine, he complained to Fred that he couldn't even do a foxtrot, much less tap dance. Fred said he was confident that he could teach *anyone* to dance. André assured Fred that his was a hopeless case—it would be a waste of time. After an hour of intensive drilling on the foxtrot, Fred finally agreed with André that not everyone could learn to dance.

I didn't go back to church until my daughters were three and five. By then, dancing had become acceptable, at least in our new church, but by then I had sat on the bandstand observing dancing for so many years that I had very little interest in it anymore.

In fact, there are very few musicians who can dance, or at least very few who confess they can. Perhaps it's because at the age when most young men are learning to dance, the musicians among them are on the bandstand playing the music everybody else is learning to dance to. I am left with the distinct impression that the ability to dance would be a kind of admission they weren't as serious about their craft as they should be.

When I was a freshman in high school, a new family, the Elders, moved into town. The husband was a dispatcher for the railroad and his wife was an outrageously funny lady. Their daughter, the classmate I mentioned before, had the same name as I but spelled hers "Bette." A lovely and accomplished girl with a great figure, Bette quickly became the most sought-after person in town. She was a skillful tap dancer—the only one in town—and played alto saxophone beautifully. She was friendly, outgoing, and everything I wanted to be. I desperately wanted to be friends with her, but as she was a grade ahead of me I knew my chances were slim.

In the end, Bette's parents and mine became close friends. I complained to my mother one day about my inability to make an impression on Bette, despite the family friendship. She asked me if Bette was aware of how much I liked her. Of course she wasn't, because I was too shy to show it. Mother gave me a piece of advice that has stood me in good stead through the years. I have handed it down to my daughters. She said that it is almost impossible not to like someone who genuinely seems to like you. The moment I demonstrated my feelings to Bette we became best friends. If she wasn't staying all night at my house, I was at hers, putting a strain on both our sets of parents as they spent half the night shouting at us to stop giggling.

We both had dreadful manufactured laughs—a quick intake of breathy sound scooping up was my laugh, while hers began at the top and scooped down. The whole town knew when the two Bettys were at the movies because we guaranteed it with our bizarre laughter. This was not the worst of it. Our two favorite expressions were "Boy howdy" and "Swell goody." We had a friend also named Betty, and as we three walked down the street, it was great sport for the townspeople to call out "Betty" in order to see three heads turn in concert.

There was nothing I'd rather do than dance. There were weekly dances in outlying towns but none in Hamburg. Every Thursday night Bette Elder's parents, my parents, and Bette and I drove to Rockport, Missouri, for the dance. All the way there we listened to the Bing Crosby show. Bette's mother was the life of the party. After the dance we all went to a diner to have a snack. The moment a sandwich appeared, Mrs. Elder would hit it with her palm. I thought it was very funny until one night my date ordered a hamburger, liberally doused it with catsup and mustard, and before he could take a bite I hit it with my palm. Catsup and mustard flew all over him!

My favorite dance was every Tuesday night in Shenandoah, Iowa. I always drove my father's car and paid my own way in. My father found this strange and expensive. I explained that I needed the freedom to dance with whomever I chose and not be stuck with "the guy that brung me." As a joke (he said) my father bought me some falsies as I seemed unable to grow my own. One week I wore them to the dance in Shenandoah. It must have come as quite a shock to my usual dance partners, seeing me with a bosom. Never mind, because with all my strenuous dancing they shifted, one to each side, so that I ended up with four bosoms! I beat a hasty retreat to the outdoor four-seater toilet and threw them overboard.

I have tried to understand why certain fellows lie about their sexual experiences, claiming to have slept with certain women when it isn't true. This particular pattern was the reason I had a terrifying couple of hours after one of my weekly dances. Two brothers from Hamburg sometimes drove to Shenandoah to the dances and would occasionally take me as passenger. After the dance we always met at a local diner for the drive home. A fellow I knew very well (from Shenandoah) drove me a couple of miles out of town for what I thought was going to be your basic necking session—I wasn't into heavy petting. (I think they called it that in those days!) No sooner had we parked when he began to get very physical with me. No problem for him as he was a football player. Somehow I struggled and held him at bay, but he wasn't giving up and I was tiring. He told me that one of our mutual friends had said he'd slept with me so why was I making such a fuss. I escaped by claiming I needed to step into the bushes for a moment and when I returned I would stop fighting. The moment I got out of the car I started running as fast as I could toward town. He drove along beside me, begging me to get in the car. He promised to leave me alone, but I didn't trust him. By the time I reached the diner, of course my ride had long since left. The football player's younger brother was in the diner, and when I told him what happened, he drove me to Hamburg, apologizing for his brother's behavior the whole way.

I must have been a rarity. Perhaps because of my father's drinking problem, I didn't drink at all. Nor did I even want to try. I can remember someone giving me a Coke laced with rum at a dance. I don't know why he thought I wouldn't know he'd spiked it. My nondrinking made me very popular with my male peers. They drove me to dances but knew that I would be sober at the end and would drive them all home. Many's the morning the phone would ring and one of the boys inquired if his car was there! In fact, my father taught me to drive by the time I was thirteen. He took me out in the country and put me behind the wheel. What could I hit? Maybe a cow!

My mother began giving me piano lessons when I was about six but I fought her every step of the way, so she sent me to a piano and voice teacher who suggested giving me singing lessons in addition to the piano. Much to everyone's surprise, I developed into a coloratura soprano. I was expected to sing in most of the high school assemblies and could see the young men wince when my name was announced. Something about "Lo, Hear the Gentle Lark" really turned them off. Anytime my father heard this particular song, he bolted. I counteracted some of this by forming a trio with two of my male classmates. To my indifferent accompaniment on piano, we sang some of the current pop songs. For these occasions, I sang in a low register, trying to sound as much like Helen O'Connell as possible.

My mother was always confident that I'd be in show biz, going so far as to have me vaccinated on the inside of my left knee so I wouldn't have a scar on my arm for all to see while wearing the glamorous evening gowns I was destined to wear.

My first year in high school my voice lessons started to pay off. I began to win a few music contests. When I was a junior in high school I sang "Si, mi chiamano Mimi" from the opera *La Bohême*, for which I won the national contest. The year before I won, Bette Elder won it, playing her alto sax. When she returned home the entire town, including the Hamburg High School marching band (in which I played bass drum), met her at the depot and escorted her up Main Street in triumph to her home.

In order to be eligible for the national contest, you had to first win a sub-district contest. Next, district, then state. Only then could you qualify for the national. After I won the requisite number of contests, thereby earning the right to compete in the national contest, the school board, in its infinite wisdom, decided that I had no chance to win The Big One so did not vote the money to send me on, as they had for Bette the year before. The high school superintendent was so outraged by this that he furnished his own car, the money, and his son to drive my teacher and me to Des Moines, where the contest was being held that year. It was an exhilarating feeling, driving back to Hamburg, having not only won the top honor, but also having proved the school board had been wrong about me.

Every Saturday afternoon a flatbed truck would be parked in the center of Main Street. (Hamburg had a population of two thousand in those days.) On it sat a young local man, playing disc jockey, spinning records, and praising the wares being offered by the local merchants. As it happened, there was a bitter rivalry between the two piano/vocal teachers in town. The young man on the flatbed happened to be a pupil of the rival teacher. As my teacher and I drove toward Main Street—in sharp contrast to the acclamation accorded Bette the year before—the young man played a record that he dedicated to me. It was called "Miracles Sometime Happen." I'll be happy to show you my scars from that little episode!

In my senior year I miraculously made the National Honor Society and was given a scholarship to Curtis Institute, a prestigious music school in Philadelphia. I was also offered a scholastic and music scholarship to Drake University in Des Moines, but I elected to stay near home. My parents were struggling to stay afloat, and I simply couldn't ask them to make the sacrifice they would have had to make to send me to Drake. Instead, I went to a business college in

Des Moines, a move that has saved my life more than once when the gigs dried up and I needed to make a living as a secretary.

At American Institute of Business (A.I.B.) I was asked to sing at a morning assembly. (My vocal teacher must have ratted!) Remembering the reaction of the young men back in Hamburg when they knew they were in for a few minutes of "serious music" and convinced that my soprano voice would cancel out all chances at dating, I invoked my Helen O'Connell persona and sang a current pop tune. The college band leader hired me for the band.

While I was in college and living about a mile from school, I used to pass a bakery on my way home, which sold day-old baked goods. I was always a terrible snob in our bakery when customers came in and bought day-old goods, but my finances were such that I was very happy to buy a dozen day-old cinnamon rolls from the Des Moines bakery. The problem was that I ate all of them, so by the time I went home for Christmas I weighed about 150 pounds. I remember my mother asking me if I happened to see her daughter at school—that's how unrecognizable I was. In the next year all the weight came off and I was back to 125. I wish I could remember how I did that!

My mother gave me a bus ticket to California for Christmas. Most of my relatives, both on my father's and my mother's side, had moved out here. Before I left she gave me a laundry lecture: wash out your underwear every night because you can't expect your aunts to do it for you. I went out quite a few times while living with one of my aunts, and every night I'd wash out my panties and hang them on a towel rack. She was so upset by this that she called my other aunt with whom I was scheduled to stay for the next week saying that she was worried sick about me and wondered if she should call her sister, my mother, as obviously I was up to no good as every night when I came in I washed out my panties. The next week my new aunt watched me very carefully and put in a call to the first aunt. She said she didn't think it was necessary to alert my mother as I had stayed in every night and still had washed out my panties!

When I got back to Hamburg, I heard that my favorite territory band was auditioning girl singers. Hamburg had an archrival town in Shenandoah, twenty-six miles away. Their inhabitants were wont to call Hamburg "the toughest town in southwest Iowa." Why this was I never found out, but when I heard the band was auditioning girl singers and that one of the local Shenandoah girls was trying out for the band, I was outraged and decided to audition if only to beat her out. After the audition the band manager told me they'd make a decision and call me.

Territory bands were almost all what they called "tenor bands." The tenor played lead. In fact there were only three tenors in the band, whereas the hipper "name" bands, with the exception of the society bands, used alto sax on top. The Royce Stoenner territory band, for which I auditioned, used four saxes with alto playing lead; it was a pretty fair band.

After an evening of strenuous jitterbugging, I looked as if I had just come out of the shower. Stoenner told me later that he was fascinated with my dance technique; if it was the custom to jump one foot off the floor, I jumped two. Drenched with sweat, I had auditioned for the band after they finished the job. I shall never forget that my audition song was "The Nearness of You," because although I don't have "perfect" pitch, I do have "relative" pitch, and for some reason this song has been a vehicle I can use to find "G," the key in which I sing the song. This is particularly useful when I'm not near a piano. I always sing this song in "G," so if I want to find any other note I sing up or down from "G." This is neither "perfect" nor "relative" pitch but somewhere in between.

It is almost impossible for an accompanist to put me in the wrong key in any tune because somehow I know how the first note is supposed to "feel" in my throat and if it feels wrong, my throat closes and I can't start singing.

Two weeks later I got a call from Stoenner telling me I was hired. In a whirlwind of activity, my mother sorted and packed my clothing, sent me off for a permanent, and drove me to Omaha the very next night where I was to join the band the following day. She bought me a couple of gowns in Omaha the next morning before depositing me at the band bus. I remember her saying about halfway between Hamburg and Omaha, "What am I doing sending my eighteen-year-old daughter off on the road to live on a bus with ten men!" She was so excited by this new opportunity for me it hadn't even occurred to her to worry until then. She needn't have.

• 2 •

Royce Stoenner

The Stoenner band was booked out of Omaha, Nebraska, and the band manager had made arrangements with a certain gas station so that when in Omaha the bus would not only be allowed to park behind the station but that an electrical hookup to the bus would be provided.

Newly permed and nicely dressed, I tapped on the bus door. The manager opened it, stared at me for a long moment and made it clear he had no idea who I was. The last time they saw me my hair was soaked with sweat, my makeup had vanished, and I looked dreadful. He warmed up considerably when I told him who I was. He told me later that, after my audition and before they decided to take a chance on me, they had a discussion about what could be done to somehow "fix me up," so they were now delighted to see that I was presentable.

The Stoenner band had never had a vocalist before, so he had lectured the band at great length to stay away from the girl singer or both she and the offending musician would be fired. I walked onto that bus and fell in love with the trombone player. He confessed that he had felt the same attraction so had crawled into one of the upper bunks so as not to be tempted to stare at me. He defeated his purpose by crawling into the one directly across from where I sat, so he could stare without my knowing it.

Living on the bus is a trying and uncomfortable way of life; but in my experience, being young and having no frame of reference other than my ancestral home, it was exciting and great fun. The girl singer develops a very special relationship with most of the band. They are very protective of her. Obviously they cannot all be her lovers, so it is not uncommon for the girl singer to find a kindred spirit on the band, and he and she are an "item" for the duration of the job. Very often the relationship is so special it ends in marriage.

The term "chick singer" is a pejorative one. I am not exactly sure why. I have known dozens of girl singers and have found the majority of them to be bright and witty. There is no question, however, that a certain stigma is attached to us.

There are some notorious members of this sorority—like the famous girl singer who for her birthday made it with the entire band. I always wondered whether that was her present to them or theirs to her.

One of my girl singer friends told me of an extremely unpleasant episode. She was with the Gene Krupa band and was having some female complaint. She later found out that someone on the band had drilled a hole in the wall separating their room from hers and invited some of the "cats" to spy on her as she treated herself. This disgusting and puerile behavior was, I hope, rare.

The Stoenner band not only traveled on the bus; we lived, washed, and slept on it. I had my own room! Just inside the bus door to the right was a small door. Opening it, you found floorspace of about thirty by thirty inches where I placed a small cardboard dresser. There was a "generous" niche between the wall and the window measuring about six inches into which I crowded my extensive wardrobe. To the left of the floorspace was my six-foot-long bunk. In order to get into it, I had to crawl about halfway down, make a U-turn, and crawl back. I am claustrophobic today and I can't help but think this experience may have made a strong contribution toward it.

In winter the blankets actually froze to the foot of the bunk. I have notoriously cold feet, so this was torture for me. During the summer my mother came into the bus to remove and wash my blankets and discovered that frost still covered the foot of my bunk and the bottom of my blankets.

As band buses for that day went, our was almost luxurious. In the main part of the bus there were stationary upper bunks. The seats below folded down into bunks at night. There was a tiny basin where we did most of our washing up. The cab of the bus was separate, and although there were no toilet facilities, there was a buzzer system that alerted the driver as to the sex of the person asking for the rest stop. If the boys needed a rest stop and we were on the road, they'd buzz once. If I needed one, I buzzed twice—which meant don't come out of the cab of the bus, it's the chick singer. I never allowed myself to dwell on the possibility that the rest of the band could have been peeking at me through the windows. It was difficult enough to expose my (relatively) innocent flanks to the occasional car driving by. In the daytime we stopped at gas stations, but often I was in big trouble because I was in my nightgown and could hardly jump out in a robe to use the restroom. Recently I ran into Rick Richardson, my old boyfriend from the Stoenner band, and he reminded me that once while I was in the ladies' room, they drove away without me. I have no recollection of this event. I assume they came back for me!

Each band member received fifteen dollars a week as salary, plus room. "Room" was the bus. Stoenner and the manager explained to me that for them to pay me the same salary as the boys might cause a riot, so they would ostentatiously pay me twelve-fifty a week and once a month slip me the extra ten, making up the difference between their salary and mine. I think that was the last time in my life when I seemed to have more than enough money. We're talking about 1940, when it was possible to have three meals a day for, perhaps, a dollar and a half.

For a little extra money two of the band members shared the driving. There was a compact storage compartment beside my quarters which had to be packed precisely or all of the instruments wouldn't fit. This was done assembly line-style with great good humor by the entire band, sans the leader and me. Stoenner and his wife traveled by car.

There was a chain of very nice ballrooms owned by one man, and it was quite a coup to be hired to play all of them. Our band had just been booked for the first time to play in all three, beginning with the Surf Ballroom in Clear Lake, Iowa. The other two ballrooms were the Turf in Austin, Minnesota, and the Prom Ballroom in St. Paul. Although I had worked a few jobs with the band before this very important one and was fairly familiar with the vocal book, I knew they would be watching the audience's reaction to me very closely. It was this kind of pressure that triggered an affliction that still haunts me from time to time. The buildup by the band about the importance of this job was so traumatic to me that my lower lip broke out in fever blisters. This unattractive (and painful) ailment occasionally plagues me to this day when I have a particularly nerve-wracking experience. Sometimes it is so severe that my chin breaks out as well. Fortunately I have a fat lower lip which, if made up carefully, overshadows the bumps, especially from behind the microphones we used in those days. (The first time I used a cordless mike I was extremely anxious. I felt exposed. Although the mikes on stands were maybe an inch in diameter, I felt comforted standing behind one. Now here I was out in the open!)

I am a strong believer in the axiom that "neatness counts," but you can forget it on the band bus. I am probably as adept at ironing a three-tiered tulle-skirted evening gown on the hotel nightstand as anyone, but we lived on the bus so that was impossible. It was decided that, since the band needed new uniforms, I should get a matching uniform with a skirt rather than trousers. These uniforms were brown covert cloth trousers/skirt worn with camel hair jackets. We wore burgundy feather boutonnieres. I have never been so proud nor felt so much a part of anything. (Well, maybe in the Hamburg High School Marching Band.) This was the era of "zoot suits," and the men's trousers were something to behold! Held up by suspenders, the trousers began at chest level. Occasionally one of the trumpet players would forget to zip his fly, and as the zippers to these trousers were about eighteen inches long, not only the lower, but most of the upper torso was exposed. It would have been a kindness to point out the oversight, but I was much too embarrassed to say anything. I was afraid he'd think I'd been staring at his crotch. In any case, my new suit was a boon, as I could hang it in my spacious closet where it stayed relatively well pressed.

The manager had a nickname. I can only spell it the way it sounded: Fee-otts. After a few weeks on the bus, feeling relaxed and part of the family, I called the manager "Fee-otts." The entire band collapsed in laughter. I was puzzled, but no one explained it to me until much, much later. It was the cleaned-up-for-the-girl-singer version of "fart," one of the dreaded "F" words that I still feel uneasy uttering. The dreaded other "F" word comes more easily these days, although at one time I never used the word out of context.

Although the band was booked out of Omaha, the entire band lived in Kansas City. To go from one city to the other there was no avoiding Hamburg, as the highway ran right through it. En route from Omaha to Kansas City they often dropped me off for a couple of days so I could get my laundry done and my feet warmed up. As we'd drive down the long street leading into Main Street in Hamburg, the band members would all hang out the window singing, "On, oh Hamburg, on, oh Hamburg, crash right through that line" (sung to "On, Wisconsin"). Someone would always shout, "Here she comes, folks, the hometown girl made good." I protested, but not so much that they'd stop doing it. We'd converge on my parents' bakery much as the locusts did in *The Good Earth*, eating everything in sight, which my parents were delighted to provide.

My mother had long since given up any hope of a career in music, so she got a vicarious thrill every time we came to town. Years later she came to visit me when I was singing in New York and insisted on viewing all the places I had described through the years so that she could picture me there when she got home again.

We spent a great deal of time in Kansas City, and Rick's parents were kind enough to invite me to stay with them each time the band came to town. By then it was obvious to everyone in the band that we were in love, but Royce made no move to fulfill his promise to fire us.

The Lunceford band played the Playmor Ballroom in Kansas City, and the entire Stoenner band went to hear it. What a great band. Trummy Young, Snooky Young, Willie Smith, and Gerald Wilson are some of the names we saw on the band.

Kansas City of course is famous for jazz. While the band was in Kansas City, we often heard the bands of Harlan Leonard and Jay McShann. This was during the time when Charlie Parker used to come into the clubs to sit in. Sometimes when I am complaining bitterly about my creaking bones, I remember that I was present during the very best of times for a jazz lover. I feel so fortunate to have been born at the time I was, so I heard these bands in person rather than only on record.

The piano player on the band was seventeen, I was eighteen, and Rick was nineteen—the "babies" of the band. Rick and I had made an agreement that, if we were ever tired of being together twenty-four hours a day and felt we'd rather be with someone else, we'd be honest about it. One heartbreaking night in Kansas City he confessed to me that that evening he would have been much happier to have hung out with the guys than be with me. I was absolutely devastated. As we had a couple of days off, I went back to Hamburg in tears. I don't know how my mother came to be so wise, but throughout the years she has given me so much wonderful advice that I have passed it all on to my children. (They didn't listen either!) This once, I did. She said that as Rick and I were, indeed, thrown together so much, it was natural that this would happen sooner or later. She suggested that, when I rejoined the band in Omaha the next day, I tell Rick that I understood his wish to "hang out" and that I agreed that we should both go our own way and see other people as well as each other. It did the trick, because that was the last time he mentioned hanging out. Thanks, Mom. (My older daughter, Claudia, told me recently that if she had taken my advice she could have avoided a lot of grief.)

The education I derived from sitting on the band bus all those years has been invaluable to me in my relationships and even in my behavior toward men. Initially, the band always edits its conversation, but eventually the girl singer becomes integrated into the group, and if she shuts up and listens, she'll learn plenty. I've never been much of a drinker, but hearing the guys in the band talking about certain females they'd taken out and plied with so many drinks that the seduction was simple has made me very wary of falling into that particular trap. I was twice as vigilant after a couple of drinks.

Max, one of the trumpet players, had only one arm. He was so relaxed and easy about it that no one felt the slightest embarrassment about razzing him. He would hang his arm on an upper bunk while he slept, and we could hear it swinging about as we drove through the night. One day I was giving manicures to some of the band members and Max suggested that I do his manicure at half price. After that I began to tease him as much as the rest of the band did. He was a very attractive man, and girls were always hanging around him during and after the job. Once he asked me if I wondered why he had so many ladies after him. I said yes. I've never forgotten that he told me it was because he had "a crooked goodie"! I'd like to have seen that.

Although my mother had always been straight with me from the beginning about where babies came from and how they were made, I never reasoned or envisioned how this could be accomplished. One night while I was still in high school I double-dated with a close girlfriend who already knew how this was achieved because she and her steady boyfriend practiced it in the backseat of the car almost nightly. The four of us were lying on two blankets several feet apart. All evening my date tried to pry my tightly clamped legs apart. Only some dim instinct led me to keep them that way. Later that night when my girlfriend and I were alone, she asked me why I was so silent. I told her that my date had tried to force my legs apart and I couldn't understand why. She burst into laughter and explained it to me. That wasn't all I didn't understand. Being an only child, I didn't have the opportunity to check out male genitalia. Apparently my father had been quite happy to be seen nude by me when I was a baby, but when I was eighteen months old and being bathed in tandem with my two-year-old male cousin, I took one look at him and said, "Just like daddy's!" That destroyed my last chance for another educational look at my father. I had, however, seen very young boys and at age eighteen still couldn't understand how such an insignificant-looking appurtenance could possibly penetrate anything. One night in the cab of the band bus, Rick carefully explained that phenomenon to me. Amazing.

My mother had prepared me far in advance for the time I would begin to menstruate by buying me all the equipment and explaining how to use it. I was so relaxed when the day came that I didn't even announce it to her. She learned of it when I asked her to buy some Kotex for me. The drugstore clerk was a male and the thought of asking *him* for Kotex was out of the question.

After I joined the band, it was my fervent hope that I could get through my period without the musicians being aware of it. However, since my cramps were so severe each month, it became impossible. I was unable to get out of my bunk one day, and the manager contacted a local doctor who came to the bus to give me a shot of morphine. He gave me a few pills which he warned me to take at least an hour before the job; otherwise, I might fall off the bandstand. Every month there was a repeat of this scene, so I soon got over my embarrassment. The euphoria I felt made it easy for me to understand addiction.

When Tommy Dorsey's band played the Surf Ballroom in Clear Lake, Iowa, our whole band went to hear it. Those were in the glorious days of Frank Sinatra, Buddy Rich, and the Pied Pipers with Jo Stafford. The band was terrific, and Tommy was one of my favorite ballad players. No one ever quite got his beautiful sound.

Our band had an arrangement of "Blue and Sentimental." One afternoon they bet me I couldn't learn the tune and lyrics by the job that night. I took up the challenge and sang it with the band that night. For years I could hear a tune once and immediately sing it. Of course, a half hour later I'd forgotten it!

We had a few arrangements in which, as I sang the song, the band sang a kind of patter behind me. I knew that something was wrong with the lyrics, but I never could quite understand what they were singing. Just as well, as the "F" word was heavily featured. Of course the audience never knew.

The day finally came when I was fired. Rick and I had gotten comfortable with the idea that our liaison was being accepted by Stoenner, so it was a great shock to me. An even greater shock was that Rick *wasn't* fired. Where was Gloria Steinem when I needed her!

I went back to Hamburg and joined a small band working around the Midwest. Within a few months Stoenner called and hired me once more. Rick had left the band and gone to New York where he put in for his New York 802 card and at the same time was studying trombone with Miff Mole.

The band went to Richmond, Virginia, for what is called a "location" gig, which was ordinarily any gig that lasted over two nights. The ballroom where we were booked for a couple of months enabled us to move out of the bus and into a boarding house.

Stoenner hired a manager because he had decided to get serious about making something more than just a territory band out of the band. The new manager told Stoenner that he was not a forceful enough first trumpet player and that in order to have a strong brass section he'd have to hire someone else to play lead trumpet. We found a first trumpet player in Texas who was willing to join the band. Before he could get on the bus for Richmond, the manager casually mentioned to Stoenner that he knew of a local first trumpet player whose wife also sang. Both could be hired for the same price being offered to the trumpet player from Texas, thereby saving my salary. I shan't keep you in suspense. I was fired again. I'll tell you one thing: If he ever calls me again. . . .

Rick suggested that I come to New York. Before I left, I had a few conversations with a girl singer in which I assured her that I would never go up to a man's hotel room. She laughed and bet me that within a month I'd be in at least a half dozen. The hotel room is the "home" of the musician on the road, so, of course, she was right, although somewhat conservative.

I was nineteen years old, had a twenty-five dollar bankroll, and knew no one in New York City except Rick, so the only logical thing to do was leave for the Big Apple immediately.

• 3 •

New York Adventures

When I informed Rick that I was coming to New York with no place to stay, he put me in touch with two women friends he'd met. I was to share an apartment at the Whitby on 45th Street. It was a one bedroom with twin beds. The arrangement was whoever came in last would sleep on the couch in the living room. My first night in New York the two generous roommates invited Rick to spend the night. We were both embarrassed at this "first" for us, but we didn't want to seem too unsophisticated, so I slept under the covers and he slept on top. This, after having known each other (in the Biblical sense) for over a year!

Some time before making my move to New York, my mother and I were waiting for a relative in the lobby of the old Cornhusker Hotel in Lincoln. We noticed a few men playing the pinball machines in the corner, and from their conversation we knew they were musicians. One of them approached us and explained that he was the manager of the Isham Jones band and they were playing a local ballroom that night and he would be happy to "comp" us if we came out. (My mother was constantly being mistaken for my sister, so this was not unusual.) We went out to hear the band, and at the end of the evening the manager, Frank Walsh, gave me his card and said I should look him up if I ever came to New York. For some reason I kept his card, although a trip to New York seemed about as remote to me at the time as a trip to Russia would have been. He may have had reason to regret his kind offer because when I got to New York I looked him up immediately.

Frank Walsh knew Joe Glaser, the famous jazz artists' representative. Glaser represented Louis Armstrong, Lionel Hampton, Billy Eckstine, Billie Holiday, and probably many more artists I have forgotten. Apparently he began as a waiter in Chicago, where he met and became friends with Louis, who encouraged him to come to New York to manage him. They never had a formal contract, just a handshake between friends. There's not a lot of that around anymore!

Frank called Joe Glaser and made an appointment with him to meet with us. Sitting in his outer office, we could hear Joe repeating over and over, "Lionel, for Christ's sake, don't sing. Lionel, for Christ's sake, don't sing!" Every time Mundell and I hear a bad singer, one of us is bound to say, "For Christ's sake, Lionel!" Of course Joe was talking to Lionel Hampton.

When Frank told Joe that he wanted to help me, Joe suggested we go to Nola Studios, a famous rehearsal hall near 51st and Broadway where Les Brown's band (also managed by Joe) was rehearsing. There I could sing a few tunes and Joe could decide if I had any talent.

Mind you, fresh from the Midwest, I hadn't even heard of Les Brown's band, so I was *entirely* without fear. We went into a huge hall where the band was set and Joe explained to Les what we wanted to do. First, Ben Homer, who was Les's arranger at the time, played piano for me while Les, Joe, and Frank listened to me on a speaker in the rear of the room. Then Les played for me while Ben listened. I could see that a lot of excitement was building about my singing. After several songs, Les told me that he wanted me to join the band! Talk about overnight success! In New York for a total of two days and already offered a job with a big-name band. It was too much!

It *was* too much. After I floated out of the studio, Joe reminded Les that, some time before, he had also been wildly enthusiastic over a jazz-oriented singer from Chicago and had hired her on the spot. When they heard her air-checks, they were appalled. She was out of tune and out of work! This had been a costly experience because she was under contract and they had to buy her out. Joe didn't want this to happen again. As a compromise, Joe agreed that they would find me another singing job and pay for lessons with Sy Oliver for a month. After that I could join the band. It turned out to be a way of letting me down easy, although Joe did set up a singing job for me at the Famous Door on 52nd Street. As for the lessons with Sy Oliver: his name was never mentioned again. Nor did I ever meet him.

I don't remember thinking of myself as a hayseed, but in retrospect, I was a reasonable facsimile. Shortly after I arrived in New York, I went to a building that contained one of the agencies handling bands, etc. As I stood in the lobby looking for the agency's location, a man came up and handed me his card. He was the representative for a stocking manufacturer. As I was vain about my legs, he had no trouble convincing me that he could employ me as a stocking model. A few days later he called me and asked to come up. I didn't know the man but some instinct told me not to be alone with him, so I asked Betty, my roommate, to be there. The man was not happy about this so I asked Betty to leave. I no longer remember the specifications for the "perfect" legs, but when the man measured mine, he said they qualified. The measuring was a little off-putting as he insisted that I put my leg on his lap to facilitate the measuring. He then told me that each year the stocking manufacturers had a contest to see whose model had the best legs. He indicated that the prize was mine if I cooperated. I asked him what he meant by "cooperate." It seems the job entailed some phone answering, some modeling, and some entertaining out-of-town buyers. I asked him what he meant by "entertaining." He said, "Do you mean would you have to get laid?" I was absolutely horrified. That side effect had never even occurred to me. Interestingly, from that day to this the word "laid" has had the most loathsome connection. I cannot bring myself to utter the word unless there is a chicken in the room.

My singing job at the Famous Door was typical of the operating policy of some of the clubs on 52nd Street. The girl singer, or singers, would sing a set and then sit with the customers—sort of a b-girl with chops. If more was expected of me than just joining a customer for drinks (which for some reason were called "downs") it was never spelled out. I didn't drink spirits, so the bartender would mix up an orange juice and God-knows-what-else concoction, fill it with fruit, and give it some exotic name. To my horror, one night one of the customers asked to taste it. I knew my cover would be blown, but somehow it wasn't. The customer couldn't tell that there was no booze in it.

The owner of the Famous Door was an extremely nice man. Eventually he allowed me to give up sitting with the customers and just sing. Sammy Price, the boogie-woogie piano player, was my accompanist. The club had various headliner acts: comedy teams, show biz belter-type singers, and once a small band fronted by a clarinetist named Nick Jerrett, who was Frances Wayne's brother. His piano player was a very young Ralph Burns. However, the star of the show, who was the owner's lady, was a stripper named Zorita. Her costar was a very large python, and the act was called "The Consummation of the Wedding of the Snake." It shouldn't be too difficult to figure out the moves in this act. The python was black, so the customers couldn't see that the snake's ability to relieve himself was thwarted by electrician's tape plastered over his alimentary canal. It seems that one of Zorita's snakes had once felt the urge during her act and had left a generous deposit on her. She kept two snakes upstairs near the dressing rooms (one as understudy?) and the odor up there was fierce. The snakes would die regularly, and I always suspected these deaths were caused by coercive constipation.

Upstairs in the dressing room I was fascinated watching the women apply their makeup. I wore pancake makeup and a little lipstick, and that was all the primping I did for my intermission singing stint. Meanwhile, Zorita and whatever ladies were currently appearing would go all out, melting black wax to apply to their eyelashes, painting on exotic mouths that bore little resemblance to their own lips' natural shape. They could barely believe my makeup job, so one night they decided to make me up. By the time they finished, no one recognized me, including me. Although the makeup job was a one-night stand, I did begin wearing mascara and painted on the obligatory exotic mouth. It took me years to break the habit.

Zorita had a good ten fur coats. I admired each one out loud. She said, if I let her take me in hand, I could have all the fur coats I wanted. I had to decline with thanks when I found out how these coats were to be won.

My two roommates were a little older and a great deal more experienced than I, so when a friend of theirs called and offered to show a couple of "dirty" movies he'd managed to borrow, they invited a group of friends up to our apartment to view them. The friend suggested to them that I was a little naive for this, but they and I assured him that this wasn't true. He set up the projector in the kitchen, shining its image on the wall in the living room. He insisted that I sit in the kitchen with him because he didn't believe for a moment that I was as worldly as I pretended. It's a good thing, too, because the film opened with an innocent shot of the seashore and a couple in bathing suits wading into the water. As they waded, they began to remove their suits. I was absolutely horrified and ran out the kitchen door into the hallway. A strange reaction because I wasn't unfamiliar with what boys and girls do. This was all the friend needed. He shut off the projector, turned on the lights, and told the eager audience in the living room that the show was off. The friend was furious with my roommates and the audience was furious with the friend and me, so they scheduled it for another night and I was sent to the movies. I have seen a few of those movies since then, and for some reason they always make me laugh. In fact, I was once thrown out of a movie theater for laughing hilariously at the stripper on the stage. I'm no longer embarrassed; I just find this kind of movie boring.

It was about this time that my singing jobs dried up and I became discouraged. I was telling a male friend my troubles when he asked me what I'd do if someone came along and offered to "make me a star" with the proviso that I sleep with him. We've all heard of "the casting couch." By now everyone knows that it isn't exclusive to the movies. I told my friend that I'd do it, a glib response that I regretted later. Sure enough, a couple of days later he called me and said he was in touch with a moneyed man who would be happy to help me, with no strings attached. I met my friend who took me to the Astor Hotel where I met the "Angel." The three of us went to his room, whereupon my friend mysteriously disappeared. The man said he'd underwrite arrangements, wardrobe, publicity, coaching—whatever it took. He said that this was not contingent upon my sleeping with him, but what would I say if he *did* ask me to sleep with him. He said, "Mind you, I'm not asking you to sleep with me, but to show me that you appreciate what I'm going to do for you, what would you say?" I assured him that I'd say yes. He then said, "All right, I do want you to sleep with me." With admirable aplomb, I rushed into the bathroom, locked the door, and began to sob. Presently my friend came up and rescued me. So much for stardom.

It does remind me of a famous girl singer who slept with a mediocre arranger in order to get free arrangements. When I heard this, I said I'd be happy to sleep with him if he promised *not* to write me any arrangements!

By now my two roommates were so disgusted with me that, when I was asked to share a small room in the same building with the aforementioned girl singer also named Betty, I accepted. Betty and I each paid seven dollars a week, and although some weeks it was a struggle, the rent was always on time. One evening when my roommate was out of town on a singing job, one of her suitors called. He was one of the more prominent saxophone players in town. He asked for Betty, and I explained that I was the wrong Betty. He insisted that I wasn't. I asked him to describe the Betty he thought he had on the phone and when he described me, I asked him to come on over. (So much for loyalty to the roommate.)

If any variations on sex were going on in Hamburg, in addition to your basic missionary position, they wisely kept it from me, so when this saxophone player, who was eighteen years old at that time, suggested performing an unnatural act on me I was horrified. Up until then, I had barely heard of such a practice and the sheer depravity of it was too much for me, so I threw him out. It was with a heavy heart that I told my roommate when she returned that she was better off without this young saxophonist as he was already a hopeless pervert. (I've come a long way, baby.)

My father had made mother and me aware of a new band to be heard nightly on a remote from Boston Post Lodge, a supper club located on the Boston Post Road between New York and Boston. (A remote is a broadcast from a ballroom as opposed to a radio studio.) The band was Glenn Miller. We became big fans. It became doubly exciting when a few years later the Miller band, now in the Air Force and stationed in New Haven, Connecticut, came to New York every week on Sunday and Monday to do a broadcast. I knew some of the musicians, so every week you can bet I was there.

Each week the Miller band had to sign out of their New Haven barracks by writing "Sunday and Monday." (The two days they'd be in New York.) One of the saxophonists was finally released from the service, and when he signed out he wrote "Sunday, Monday, and Always," the title of a pretty pop tune from those days.

It was about this time that I met an extremely handsome young actor. After a few dates he suggested I come to his apartment and he'd make dinner. He thought that "tonight's the night" and I thought no such thing. After dinner he made his move. I was outraged! I grabbed my coat, stalked to the door, and left. My problem was it was his closet door. I stood there for a couple of minutes wondering how to get out of a truly humiliating situation. As I reviewed my options I began to giggle, then to howl with laughter. I came out to find he was laughing too. It saved the evening. (Though, unfortunately, not for him.)

The Chock Full 'O Nuts at the corner of Broadway and 49th was where I had lunch. A cream cheese and nut sandwich on date bread and a chocolate milk were fifteen cents. A favorite place for dinner was the Professor's, an Italian restaurant off Eighth Avenue, where an order of spaghetti was twenty-five cents—thirty-five with meatballs. I could rarely afford the deluxe dinner with meatballs. Occasionally, finances permitting, I would cross the street to the Turf restaurant where I'd stand outside eating their spectacular cheesecake. Standing was a must. It would have been unthinkable to go inside and sit down. I was never able to discover why it was mandatory to eat outside. Maybe it was because it was across the street from the Forest bar where *all* the cats hung out. (Some unwritten "hip" law, perhaps?)

In those days we all hung out in the bar at the Forest Hotel, 49th between Broadway and Eighth. What an incredible thrill it was for me to be on the periphery of a group of musicians whom I'd driven hundreds of miles to hear when I was in high school. I was in the bar under false pretenses because I still didn't drink. One afternoon a couple of us girl singer types were waiting for one of their husbands to arrive. He was very late and when he finally arrived and before his wife could excoriate him, he told her of some marijuana called Red Cross that had arrived in town and was dynamite. (It was later made famous by the Charlie Parker composition "Red Cross," which may have been named for a Parker friend, Bob Redcross.) The husband suggested we all go up to their room and smoke. I went along as an observer, and since I didn't smoke, I declined. They insisted, so I took a couple of hits. I looked into the mirror and saw a complete stranger. I was absolutely freaked out. I left with one of my friends, and as we came to the front door of the Forest, I looked to the left and saw a huge crowd of people coming for *me*. I began running down 49th Street toward Broadway with my friend in hot pursuit. She patiently explained that Madison Square Garden had just let out and these people were coming *from* there, not *for* me. Later as we stood for a moment at the entrance of an Italian restaurant waiting to be seated, I could clearly hear the conversations of the people sitting in the rear of the room.

Although I have tried to smoke pot a few times since, that was the only time I ever really got high. In fact, I've turned it down so much that the few friends I have who still smoke it don't even ask me anymore. However, there was a brief spell there when I baked a few outstanding brownies and loved every escalating minute of it. This led to an interesting incident. During my brief Alice B. Toklas days I encouraged Mundell, my husband, to eat half a brownie with me. He always declined, saying he'd smoked his share of marijuana in the old days. Finally, just before dinner one night he agreed. He had been with the Sauter-Finegan band and was and is a dedicated fan of Bill Finegan's arrangements. I had owned an album by singer

Sam Fletcher with arrangements by Bill Finegan. On it was a beautiful song called "That Sunday, That Summer." My album somehow disappeared, and I was elated when it turned out Mundell had the same album. It led to his suspicion that I was only after him for his Fletcher album! At any rate, we were both very familiar with the arrangement, having heard it dozens of times. This particular evening, having eaten our brownie, we decided to listen to "That Sunday, That Summer" on the Fletcher album. Halfway through, we looked at each other in astonishment! We heard a beautiful flute passage in the arrangement that we'd never heard before. We agreed that we *both* heard it. What's even more interesting is that once we came down from the high, we never heard that flute passage again, although we tried dozens of times.

There's something wonderful about being young. There I was in New York, out of work, barely enough money to pay the rent, and not at all apprehensive about the future. However, the singing jobs had dried up completely, and I knew that it was a great sacrifice for my parents to send me money to live on each week. I decided to go back to Omaha. My parents sent me a bus ticket. When I arrived in Omaha, I couldn't remember my parents' address or phone number. I had completely blocked it out although I had written and called them many times. In addition, I had only a few pennies on me. What a dilemma. I got into a cab and explained my problem, and the driver agreed to try to find the place. I knew it was across the street from a medical school, the name of which I miraculously remembered. It was bitter cold and snowing. The cab driver had to hang around because I couldn't pay him until I found my parents. I actually walked up to every house on the block and shouted my mother's name. Thank God she heard me and came out to rescue me.

Back in Omaha I took a job singing with Freddie Ebener's band. I sang on some jingles and did a few broadcasts at radio stations WOW and KOIL. By then, I wanted to return to New York, so I took a job in a defense plant, working the swing shift, in order to earn enough money to survive in the Big Apple.

I actually enjoyed my job in the defense plant. Very little was accomplished on our shift. The plant was making B26Cs, and some nights when they wanted to check out some of the electrical equipment they'd let me sit in the nose while they did their tests. There was a very handsome flyer attached to the Air Force and stationed at the plant. I made the mistake of dating him a few times, which led to a very painful experience. The girls in his office must have been jealous because I can think of no other reason for their cruel trick. They called my office and said they were planning a party and wondered if I'd sing at it. When I accepted, they said I'd have to sing a couple of songs over the phone—kind of an audition. I thought I'd left my naivete behind when I left Hamburg, but clearly I hadn't. I sang a couple of songs and they said they'd get back to me. I learned later that their whole office was in on the joke and they had a good laugh on me. Betty Bennett, girl singer, a.k.a. patsy!

While in Omaha my friends and I hung out at a downstairs jazz club. They booked great acts in the room, including Bobby Short and the King Cole Trio. One of my friends and I got to know the owner—the first of a long list of club owners named Murray. Big bands used to come through Omaha to work the Orpheum Theater, and invariably the band would hear about the jazz club and come down after the last show.

While the Tommy Dorsey band was in town, the King Cole Trio was appearing at the club. My girlfriend told someone in the Dorsey band that I was a singer. They in turn asked Nat Cole who graciously agreed to accompany me.

The next night when my friend and I tried to enter the club, Murray fixed me with a look of disgust and said, "We don't want your kind in here." I made him repeat this because it was beyond my immediate comprehension. I had to be helped up the stairs to the sweet evening air. My friend went back down to ask Murray his reason for barring me. He said it was because I had sung with the "nigger" band. That was over fifty years ago and it still sickens me. It was my first experience with bigotry and I only wish it had been my last.

A black couple with a young son lived in Hamburg briefly. I don't remember ever hearing either of my parents use the dreaded "N" word. I asked them exactly what this family did for a living. It would have been funny had it not been so predictable for those days. The father worked at the barber shop shining shoes, the mother cleaned houses, and the son took tap lessons and became a wonderful dancer. That was about all that was available for black people then. I admire their bravery for trying to live in a prejudiced town. I wondered if it had changed, but when I returned for my fiftieth high school reunion in 1989, I heard at least two of my classmates refer to "niggers." I was thoroughly ashamed of myself for not speaking up, especially since my best friend in high school, who has lived in California for fifty years, very quietly told one of them that he shouldn't use that ugly word. Hooray for her.

Lee Castle, a former member of the Tommy Dorsey band, had organized a band and asked me to work Loew's State Theater on Broadway. My "big break" at last. I haunted Loew's State and saw the same movie three days in a row, knowing that at the break I would see my name on the screen. Two days before the opening the theater manager told Lee that he'd have to let me go. It seems they had a surfeit of females on the bill—a girls' singing trio and two girl jugglers—so they told Lee to hire a boy vocalist. I was devastated and furious. One of my savvy friends told me he was sure I could sue the theater because they had been advertising me for a week. When I told Lee I was considering it, he begged me not to do it because he had almost ruined himself a few years before when a similar thing happened to him on Dorsey's band. Not only did he alienate himself from Tommy, but after Tommy told the story around, it took Lee a long time to rebuild his reputation among other bandleaders.

Someone introduced me to Milt Page, a young man who played piano and organ wonderfully. We began to rehearse and he booked a few gigs for us around town and in nearby New Jersey. This led to his organizing the Milt Page Quartet. The bass player, guitarist, Milt, and I formed a vocal quartet, making us both a vocal and instrumental group. The guitarist and I also sang solo.

Our first big job together was for the entire summer at the Five Hundred Club in Atlantic City, New Jersey. We worked the midnight to six a.m. shift. We all lived in a small hotel next door to the club, and if I've ever been happier during a summer, I can't remember it. After work ended at six, we'd have breakfast, change clothes, rent bicycles, ride up and down the boardwalk, sun ourselves for a couple of hours, and then go back to the room to sleep. When we awakened, we had dinner and milled around until time for our midnight shift.

In back of the club was the gambling room, and every weekend some of the horse-playing, gambling types would come down from Philadelphia. Our playoff on the bandstand was stolen from the WJZ New York station ID: a poignant, beautifully harmonized five notes to which we added our signature ("This is the Milt Page Quartet") when the set ended. Some of the gamblers whom we came to know and love told us that during the week, back in Philadelphia standing around the pool table, a few of them would throw their arms around each other's shoulders and sing, "This is the Milt Page Quartet." It must have been a funny sight and probably sound as well.

I was musing some twenty years later about what I could have been doing with myself while the trio was playing, because of course I didn't sing every song. The Five Hundred Club had a circular bar and we were trapped in the middle of it, so there was no walking off the bandstand. One night Johnny Mandel said to my then-husband, "I used to go hear your old lady when she shook one maraca with this quartet in Atlantic City. She had good time." How could I have forgotten that I was the rest of the rhythm section?

By the time the summer ended, I had made enough contacts to be able to find a singing job with Georgie Auld's band. At my first rehearsal with Georgie's band one afternoon, sitting in the corner studying the arrangements, I heard a voice say, "You sure got some crazy laigs." I looked up and met Dizzy Gillespie for the first time. Through the years I was always delighted to see Dizzy, and if he was playing anywhere near, I went to hear him. One of the great thrills of my life was when he had the group with Charlie Parker at the Three Deuces on 52nd Street. He was completely outrageous and made me laugh a lot. I came into the Deuces one night on a date with a Marine from the Deep South. The minute Dizzy heard the Marine's southern accent he pretended that he and I were an item. The Marine stomped out and good riddance!

I happened to be in Chicago and saw that Dizzy was with Billy Eckstine's band at a black theater on the south side. I was sitting about five rows back when I suddenly saw Dizzy waving wildly at someone in the audience. I looked around several times and nobody seemed to be responding. I couldn't believe that he could actually distinguish me in that dark theater. Finally I pointed to myself and he gestured for me to come backstage. Somehow, given my humble beginnings, I could never believe that I was actually friends with the musicians who were my idols. Chubby Jackson said it the best: What a fantastic break to have been born at a time that produced the very best in jazz. Big bands were in their heyday. Prez, Dizzy, Bird, Zoot, Al, Stan, all of whom have left an incredible legacy of music.

In the late '50s when I was living in Beverly Hills, I had a phone call one day from Dizzy. He was at Norman Granz's office, which was about a mile south of my house. Dizzy was doing one of those Jazz at the Philharmonic tours for Norman, and he happened to be in town. When he heard my house was only a mile away, he said he'd be right up. Shortly after, the doorbell rang. There stood Dizzy and his bass player. Dizzy was carrying a large watermelon under his arm. I ushered him into the kitchen where my housekeeper and he cut up the watermelon, and he, the bass player, and my housekeeper sat down to eat it. I stood in the doorway in disbelief, laughing like mad. I said, "So it's all true. It really is your native fruit!"

Georgie Auld was a very handsome, very good tenor saxophonist with an excellent band. I was alternately frightened and fascinated by him. Occasionally Georgie would call my room very late at night and demand that I come to his room. I always said "no" whereupon he would tell me that a well-known singer (who shall remain nameless) would be happy to come to his room. I suggested that, in that case, he should call her.

I well remember the first stage show with Georgie. He announced me and kicked off the introduction to my song, and I came tripping out. "Tripping" was the operative word because I fell over about five microphone lines!

I wasn't too surprised when Georgie fired me. Actually, he is partly responsible for an ironclad rule I made for myself many years ago: never get involved with the leader or the club owner. Some time after that I ran into Manny Albam, a wonderful arranger, who had written for and played in Georgie's band when I was in it. When I identified myself, he said, "Oh yeah, you were the chick singer who cried all the time."

Back in New York, disillusioned with the music business, I found a job working for a song publisher in the Brill Building, 1690 Broadway, home of most of the established song publishers. The bandleader Hal McIntyre came into the office one day, and I told him I was through with show business. He said I shouldn't judge all bandleaders the same, for not all of them were like Georgie. (My basic problem with Georgie was that I sort of wanted to break my rule and say yes.)

Sid Lorraine, my employer, knew of my lurid past as a girl singer, and he couldn't believe that I could take shorthand or type. The day he interviewed me he asked me to take a letter. Then, thinking it would throw me, he asked me to read it back. I did. I think I took a total of six letters and read them back to him before he was convinced that I could handle the job. Some of the song pluggers would drop by to talk to me occasionally. Sid had the couch taken out to discourage this kind of behavior.

Although I was (barely) making enough money to live on, I wasn't singing and I missed my parents, who were then living in Long Beach, California. I was longing to go home, but as I had begged Sid Lorraine to give me the job as his secretary and then, barely two months later, wanted to quit, I lacked the courage to face him. My mother had the answer. She sent me a telegram that read: "Mother in hospital. Come west as soon as possible." She felt so guilty about this lie that she actually went to a local hospital and stood for a moment in the lobby, then went to send the telegram with a clear conscience!

• 4 •

"We Are the Waves of the Navy"

My mother was a fiercely patriotic woman and seemed almost apologetic that she didn't have a son to give to the war effort, even though she and my father both worked in a defense plant that built ships. As a result of her patriotic fervor, one day as we were passing a Navy recruiting office, I idly suggested that we go in and see about my joining the Navy. The recruiting office gave me a date a month later to be in Los Angeles for the various tests I would undergo, and I went away with a very happy mother. Somehow it never occurred to me that this was real. During the next couple of weeks I began to regret my rash promise, and on the morning I was to take the train to Los Angeles, I hoped and prayed that my mother would not awaken me. But of course she did.

In Los Angeles, after several hours of aptitude tests, physical exams, etc., I was ushered into the office of the Ensign in Charge. She said that they didn't often have recruits of my caliber—by this I assume she meant my musical ability—and she asked me if I was trying to escape something. In fact, I was. I had been involved with a married man, and a forced separation seemed to me to be the only way that gave me the courage to finish the relationship. I assured the ensign that I wasn't trying to escape.

Most of the hopefuls didn't even make it to the ensign's office but were told they would be notified if they were accepted. In my case, the ensign asked me to raise my right hand, which I did, and she swore me in! She also told me that I would never be sorry I had joined the Waves and she was absolutely right. I look back on my time in the Navy as a wonderful adventure. (Although sometimes during boot camp, slogging through the slush before the sun came up, I questioned the validity of her statement!)

It was then 1945, and along with the other recruits I was traveling on a special train that took us to New York. Boot camp was at

Hunter College in the Bronx in New York City. As short hair was required, I had had my long locks cut very short before I left California and was sporting a tight, hateful permanent. We were not allowed out of the barracks for the first few weeks so my hair was just beginning to look nice again. I was looking forward to my first weekend pass, to say nothing of my first weekend "pass." The day before it came, they chopped off my hair again!

Although boot camp was one long round of marching and waiting, I found a few kindred souls in my platoon. We slogged along in the darkness before dawn, moaning and groaning, but generally took it in stride (if you'll pardon the expression). Oftentimes we'd be standing, waiting for the next order, and it would start to pour with rain. There was no independent decision to put on your havelock (a plastic cover that fit over your hat and covered your collar so rain would run off it rather than into your uniform). Nevertheless we had to wait until our platoon commander gave us a specific order to don our havelocks. By then it was almost too late. We were soaked.

We learned to make our cots with square corners, always with the threat that the officers might try to bounce a fifty-cent piece off it. The fluffy dust balls that collect under furniture were called "kitties," and God help you if the inspector found any. You were given demerits that had to be worked off. I no longer remember why I got my demerits, but my punishment consisted of washing down the walls of a very large room, along with my fellow criminals. As we worked, I kept up a running commentary about our task. How did I know that one of the officers was standing behind me and heard every word. It came as no particular surprise that the next week I could be found busily washing down another wall!

We were billeted in some apartment buildings surrounding Hunter College campus. Two bedrooms, two women per room. One of my roommates insisted on using the glass I used when I brushed my teeth. She had gingivitis, so of course I contracted it too. Treatment was pretty basic! The dentist painted my gums with purple permanganate. I went to the commissary where the Blue Jacket band (the swing band attached as ship's company to boot camp) was having coffee. When they greeted me, I gave them a very large, startling, purple grin.

One day I needed to have a wisdom tooth pulled. While the platoon stood outside waiting, the dentist pulled my tooth and sent me back to continue the drill. None of your coddling there. I simply spat blood into the snow until my gum stopped bleeding. Oh well, it made a man of me.

Boot camp was six weeks long, but the last two weeks the training was ostensibly over and we were given jobs on the base for the two remaining weeks, joining the regular ship's company. There was a lot of resentment toward me from the other boots when I was given a job as receptionist for the photography shop. Some of the other jobs were in the basement of the building and involved arising at dawn, donning galoshes, and standing in an inch of water peeling potatoes, carrots, and whatever else was planned for the daily poisonous rations. Meals largely consisted, it seemed to me, of mutton thinly disguised as everything! The rest of the boots washed dishes, filled trays, and bussed dishes. It's no wonder my fellow boots resented me, dressed neatly in my uniform, clean and dry.

One event during boot camp stands out. When I first arrived in California, I looked up Donnie Brehm, a drummer whom I'd met at a gig in the Midwest. It turned out that he had a roommate by the name of Barney Kessel. Mother and I would go to their rooming house, and Barney would sit on one twin bed playing accompaniment for me while my mother and Donnie sat on the other and listened. Barney later hired me to work every Tuesday night at the Suzie Q, a nightclub in Hollywood. It was my only gig. He was also doing casuals and record dates around town.

By the time I was in boot camp, Barney had already toured with the Chico Marx band and was fast becoming the well-known guitarist he is today. He was appearing at the Strand Theater on Broadway with Artie Shaw's band. One day at what we laughingly called lunch, someone came to me to say that there was a visitor in the lounge to see me. Was I allowed to get up and leave just then? No, lunch was twenty minutes, and twenty minutes would pass before they would let me go see my visitor. It was Barney! I must have been a glorious sight. Until we got out of boot camp, we had to wear lisle stockings that tended to bag at the knees. To think that Barney had taken the subway before the first show at the Strand and had waded through all the red tape to see me was above and beyond the call of duty! What a gent! There's no adequate way I could thank him, although through the years I've tried.

It was during the final two weeks of boot camp that we had our interviews with the base psychologist. She asked me what I hoped to do now that boot camp was over. I said that I had heard that being a yeoman (secretary) in Washington, D.C., was the worst duty you could get, and I begged her not to send me there. Or, if she must send me there, could I somehow be connected to the music division? Alternatively, if she could arrange for me to be stationed in New York City, I'd happily become a yeoman. She seemed quite sympathetic to my fears, and I felt she would recommend one of these alternatives.

We anxiously awaited the posting of the billets, due in a week. When the day came, I read my posting with disbelief! Yeoman, Washington—the very thing I dreaded. I rushed back to the photography shop in tears and told the two ship's company photographers where I'd been posted. They said I couldn't just tell the psychologist I didn't want to be a yeoman in Washington. I'd have to have a very good reason for why I didn't want to be stationed there. After all, they said, she must know that no one *wants* to be a yeoman in Washington. After a brief consultation, they figured out what I should do: make another appointment with the psychologist and tell her there was a good reason I didn't want to be stationed in Washington: a part of my family was living there with whom I had strained relations and to be transferred there would cause me great emotional stress. I couldn't be responsible for what might happen. (In fact, one of my favorite uncles was stationed in Washington.)

I had my appointment with the psychologist where I duly explained my dilemma. When I returned to the barracks later that day and looked once again at my name, I saw that a line had been drawn through "yeoman, Washington," and "unassigned" was substituted. Some time later I heard that there was such a glut of yeomen that many were set to work peeling potatoes once again. Bless those photographers, wherever they are!

I have been a life-long Democrat and was an avid supporter of FDR. I well remember the day he died. Boot camp had ended and we were all marking time until our transfers. When the news came over the PA system at boot camp, I think our entire company cried off and on for days.

The Navy put on a weekly coast-to-coast radio show called "Waves on Parade," which featured famous guests and a terrific Navy band. The show was directed by Earle McGill, a well-known and respected director at CBS. He donated his time each week to the production and direction of the show. Ray Charles, the arranger for Perry Como and more recently responsible for the perfectly tailored music on the *Muppet Show*, was the bandleader and in charge of deciding which of the two Wave singers already in ship's company would be performing on the show. There was a third Wave who was the mistress of ceremonies.

Every week during boot camp it was quite a thrill for us to attend the broadcast and to sing the theme, "We Are the Waves of the Navy." Some time during boot camp a special night was planned for the boots, and anyone with talent was asked to perform. I sang a couple of tunes with the band, and Ray Charles was generous with his praise.

A couple of days after the "Unassigned" notice went up after my name, I was called into the large auditorium where the radio show took place. A long table was set up in the middle of the stage, and several people were sitting around it, including the writers, the two Wave singers, and Ray Charles. Earle McGill introduced himself, handed me a script, and asked me to read the lines for the mistress of ceremonies. Her job was to introduce the musical numbers, all couched in nautical terms, then read a long page each week on the activities of the men and women in the Navy around the world. He taught me how to mark my script, and it went well for what I assumed was an afternoon's diversion. After reading through the script a couple of times, we were told to take a thirty-minute break. At the end of that time I was called back to the stage to see that the auditorium was filled with hundreds of boots. Being none too swift, I still didn't understand that I had, in fact, been auditioning for the mistress of ceremonies job and was about to go on the air. Had I known, I would have been in a complete panic, as Earle knew. In the end, the radio show went off perfectly. Only afterward did they tell me that I was the new mistress of ceremonies. I was replacing a married Wave who had become pregnant and wanted out of the Navy. The former mistress of ceremonies had a British accent and it was decided to replace her with someone who had no regional accent. That landed me the job. (It's a good thing the word "wash" never appeared in the script because although I pronounce it properly now, for years I said "warsh." So much for having no regional accent.)

Why Ray Charles had asked them to try me when his only prior knowledge of my ability was when he had accompanied me on the boot show will remain a mystery. Doing that weekly show—the last fifteen minutes of which my mother heard in California—was another high point of my life.

The next week, having had seven days to contemplate the enormous responsibility that I thought was now being placed upon me, I was a bundle of nerves at rehearsal. During the show, four of us performed a skit. At one point I forgot to read my line and there was a pause, finally filled by one of the other Waves who quickly jumped in with my line. I sensed that my new-found career was going to be brief. Earle, however, was very calm and said he had expected it. The first week I sailed through because I didn't know what was coming. When I did, it would take a couple of weeks for me to settle down.

Earle directed a weekly show at CBS starring John Daly called "A Reporter's Report to the Nation," and as part of my education for the Wave show, he invited me down every Saturday to watch the rehearsal and stay through the show. He hoped that I would be able to get the feel of what he wanted out of me by seeing the way John handled the show. In it, actors dramatized real events taking place during the war. It was a slick and interesting program after which he and John Daly took me to lunch in a Swiss restaurant across the street from CBS. I am a compulsory punster, and John Daly and I used to make just enough dreadful puns to keep Earle groaning during the entire lunch.

Charlie's Tavern in midtown Manhattan was the musicians' hangout. I loved being a part of the "in" group. I always wore my Navy uniform, which prompted one of the musicians to say to me, "I can't believe it! I was drafted but you just went down and gave yourself up!"

The officer in charge of the band and singers was Lieutenant Lou Mindling. He'd worked for a booking agency before his commission, and as he'd been kind of a gofer there, he seemed bent on getting even with some of the more prominent band members for whatever indignities he'd suffered at the agency. I had the misfortune of being assigned to him as his secretary. He made my life hell and I was terrified of him. He would regularly shout "seaman" every time he wanted me. After the first couple of times I automatically carried my Kleenex box with me because invariably I was sobbing when I left. Once he opened our little discussion by saying, "Seaman, I know what you've been doing so you may as well confess." I couldn't think of a thing and said so. He said, "If you don't tell me, I'll see to it that you get a bad conduct discharge." In tears, I reiterated my innocence. The band told me that that was a technique of his. If I *had* been doing something wrong and admitted it, he had me. If not, he lost nothing. I, however, was always on the brink of a nervous breakdown. Years later when I was singing with Claude Thornhill, he came in as a civilian and told everyone how fond he had been of me. Go figure.

The two other singers, Dona Mason and Rosemary Schlack, not only sang on the show every week, but they were also the copyists for the arrangements used by the band. Lt. Mindling seemed very reluctant to have me sing on the show, but finally Ray Charles wore him down and I began to sing every few weeks in addition to my weekly mistress of ceremonies duties.

When boot camp is over, the boots are given the rank of Seaman Third Class, equivalent to Buck Private in the army. As I always opened the radio show by saying, "This is Wave Seaman Betty Bennett," it was felt that to add "third class" would diminish my clout so I received an instant promotion to seaman, which implies first class—equivalent to sergeant. I have kept some of my old scripts and here is a sample of the opening of "Waves on Parade."

ANNOUNCER:	COLUMBIA presents—SERVICE TIME:
MUSIC:	THEME UP—BAND AND SINGING PLATOON—FADE UNDER—
ANNOUNCER:	Up anchor and set sail for a great show. It's time for WAVES ON PARADE: Direct from the Little Theater of the United States Naval Training School for WAVES, in New York—COLUMBIA brings you a half hour of music by the Navy Blue Jacket Dance Band . . . the 40-voice WAVE Singing Platoon—the latest world news Harry Marble reporting—and a first hand report of Jap suicide planes in the Pacific from Lieutenant Frank.
MUSIC:	THEME UP AND OUT WITH APPLAUSE
SEAMAN BENNETT:	'Afternoon, mates: Fall in for another thirty minutes of music and up-to-the-minute news about "Uncle Sam's girls in Navy Blue." This is WAVE Seaman Betty Bennett speaking for some of the proudest girls in the world—girls who are lucky

enough to serve in the uniform of the United States Navy.'

And just a sample of one of my introductions for the Blue Jacket band:

SEAMAN BENNETT: Our musician crew sight some jive, and prepare to swing same—better scuttle all your Monday blues—because here comes a Navy Blue cargo of cheer in "I NEVER KNEW."

There were some well-known players in the Blue Jacket band. Trombonist Lou McGarrity, alto saxophonist and singer Johnny McAfee, Bobby Parks (who had a successful society band before and after the war), and Rusty Dedrick, who joined Claude Thornhill after he left the Navy. In fact, he was in the Thornhill band when I later joined it.

The radio show was a salute to the Navy and a recruiting device. When the war in Europe ended, so did the show, and the musicians who had enough points to be discharged were happy to oblige. The rest of us were attached to the Navy Liaison office at 90 Church Street, where we reported each day to study the bulletin board. Posted there were the names of those of us who were entertaining in surrounding Navy, Marine, and Army hospitals that day.

The entertainment pool at 90 Church Street consisted of jugglers, tap dancers, singers, musicians, and comics, all of whom were marking time until they collected the necessary points for discharge. Harry Babbitt, Norman Paris, Ray Charles, and Billy Reed (who later opened the posh Little Club on the East Side) were all in this group. One day when we reported for assignments, there was a note on the bulletin board from one of our departed shipmates. It read: "Here is my home phone number in California. Please call me if you're in town, and if a woman answers, hot damn!"

When VJ day came, news of it reached us as we were returning to Manhattan on a ferry after having entertained a group of veterans at St. Albans Naval Hospital on Staten Island. It was like a movie. An accordion miraculously appeared, and the passengers moved forward, singing and shouting. We all had to be herded aft by the captain because the ferry was perilously close to capsizing with the weight of all the revelers concentrated in the bow. When asked if I did overseas duty during World War II, I always say I had 160 minutes sea duty aboard the Staten Island ferry.

The Marines had a highly successful touring show called "Tars and Spars," so someone conceived the idea of imitating it with a show composed of Navy talent. We called it "Your Navy Date." Rosemary Schlack, Dona Mason, Billie Shipley, Patti Scudder, and I were the ladies of the chorus. Ray Charles, a comic/dancer called Hal Abbott, and a six-piece band completed our cast. Billy Reed was our director, and we rehearsed the show in New York City and premiered it in Washington, D.C., for the Navy brass.

Rosemary Schlack sang "I Wanna Get Married," complete with bridal gown. She delivered the lyrics with such dry humor that she stopped the show nightly. Dona Mason sang a beautiful ballad; Billie Shipley sang "I'm Just a Girl Who Cain't Say No" and was such an adorable blonde she also stopped the show. Pat Scudder was our comedienne/dancer and got a huge share of laughs.

Ray Charles suggested I sing "Do it Again," a lovely but suggestive ballad written by George Gershwin and Buddy DeSylva. It got a great response from the Washington audience which was made up of Navy personnel, but the Admiral's wife decided it had to go because it was too titillating for the troops. For the rest of the tour I sang a nice, current pop tune that was greeted pleasantly ("It's Been a Long, Long Time," a very popular tune during the war). It was no show stopper like "Do It Again" had been. I was greatly disappointed when that tune was vetoed because, although the audience reaction was good, it was nothing like the response given to the other Waves' tunes. (Okay, I was jealous!) To make it interesting (to myself) and because I was already a jazz-influenced singer, I changed the melody, improvising over the basic chords. It was foolhardy of me, as the audiences were not sophisticated as those in New York and probably wondered what happened to the melody!

Hal Abbott was the funny man master of ceremonies of the show. As we were rehearsing in New York, Billy Reed worked out a conga dance which consisted of Ray Charles, Pat Scudder, Hal Abbott, and me. I protested violently that I wasn't that kind of dancer, but I was outvoted, so every night in a ruffly costume I made a complete ass of myself doing the conga.

We traveled up and down the east coast, performing "Your Navy Date" for soldiers, sailors, and marines. We all had long hair and were always a little out of uniform which made us unpopular in whatever barracks they billeted us. We also did hundreds of hospital ward shows. They were my greatest pleasure, although frequently heartbreaking because we often performed in the plastic surgery wards, as well as the paraplegic wards. We all tried to hide our tears from the men.

After a few months on the road most of our band had collected enough points to be mustered out, so "Your Navy Date" came to an abrupt halt.

• 5 •

Claude Thornhill

While we were attached to the Navy Liaison office, we were billeted at Manhattan Towers at 72nd and Broadway, the hotel made famous by Gordon Jenkins's very popular "Manhattan Towers Suite." Aside from a few ward shows we were on our own and took full advantage of being in New York City. Although it was forbidden for the military to go uptown, my roommate and I would take off our Navy hats and jackets and make our way to the Apollo Theater. There was never any problem.

After Glenn Miller's death, Tex Beneke took over the band, and their first gig was the Capitol Theater on Broadway. I was acquainted with some of the musicians from having gone to their weekly radio shows in New York. They suggested that, if I could get out of the Navy, it would be a wonderful gimmick to have an all ex-service band that included the girl singer. I had been in the Navy one year by then and was very far from having enough points to escape. It was doubly frustrating because there was so little to do. I doubt if we did two hospital or ward shows a week. We were all marking time, waiting to collect enough points to get out. Every week another lucky sailor left. It was at this time that someone told me that if I married an ex-serviceman I could get out of the Navy within ten days. If I was conscious of this when I married for the first time, I wasn't aware of it. As (bad) luck would have it, I didn't get out in time to join the Miller band at the Capitol. They hired a civilian!

Larry Bennett, a bass player who was a close friend of mine, had been in the Army in Europe for most of the war, and when he returned to New York he called me and asked if I had heard any good bass players. I took him to hear a bass player at the Three Deuces on 52nd Street. A couple of nights later Larry took me to the Hickory House to hear a bass player he said would put mine to shame. The bass player was Iggy Shevak. We were casually introduced that night. A couple of days later I saw him again at Charlie's Tavern, a local musicians' hangout in midtown Manhattan. When he said hello, I had no idea who he was until he reminded me that Larry had introduced us at the Hickory House. Iggy's real name was Robert Coleman Shevak, but he'd been nicknamed "Iggy" after a cartoon character. He told me that he had worked with a leader who drank heavily and would use the phrase from the cartoon that was "Iggy, keep an eye on me." The nickname stuck.

A week later when my date hadn't called as he was supposed to, I was furious and decided not to wait but go to a movie. I was standing at the box office of the Winter Garden theater, frustrated at having been told by the ticket seller that the next feature was twenty minutes away, when Iggy and a friend came up Broadway. They suggested I kill the twenty minutes by having a drink with them. As we chatted, Iggy asked me why I had never married. I guess at twenty-four I was considered "over the hill." I said I hadn't had the nerve and if a wedding date were set I'd probably panic and skip town. The only way I could see myself marrying would be spur of the moment. Someone would propose, and we'd leave immediately for the Justice of the Peace. It seems incredible but he proposed and I accepted. His friend called his lady friend, and we borrowed a car and drove to Maryland where there was no three-day wait for the blood tests to clear as there was in New York. We located a very old doctor who gave us each a life-threatening blood test after which we found a Justice of the Peace. After he married us, he said, "Young man, you may kiss the bride." So help me, I said, "But I hardly know him!" Despite this bizarre beginning, the marriage lasted a couple of years.

Iggy had been in the Army so, as advertised, when I married him I was eligible to be released. Claude Thornhill had just gotten out of the Navy and had reorganized his band. He hired Iggy on bass. From rehearsal, Iggy called me to say they were auditioning girl singers. I asked my old friend and former boss Milt Page to accompany me on piano, and we rushed over, quickly did three tunes, and split. I got the call later that I was hired. Leonard Vannerson, the manager, told me that it wasn't so much my singing talents as it was the professional way I handled myself during the audition. Apparently the other singers had dithered about what to perform, or didn't know their keys, and this really annoyed Claude and the two arrangers, Bill Borden (who wrote the ballad arrangements) and Gil

Evans. I learned a little lesson that day that has paid off many times since. I am an accomplished auditioner.

So at last my little high school fantasy became a reality: I was singing with Claude Thornhill. He was a gentle, though sometimes off-the-wall man. I was intimidated by him through no fault of his own. For some reason I am always intimidated by people in positions of authority. (I prefer to think of myself as being highly sensitive, rather than threatened.) It was certainly a joy to sit on the bandstand and hear the band. Gil Evans's arrangements were marvels of invention but were so complex they had to be rehearsed on several occasions before they could be played.

There are some powerful cliques in bands, but the most powerful one I have ever had to deal with was in the Thornhill band. This clique exerted such tremendous influence over Claude that they were able to make nearly all of the major decisions for him. Perhaps Claude was just content to play the piano.

The members of the clique were all first-class players who could make life miserable for any member who didn't fit in, no matter how well that person played. They were constantly on the lookout for an excuse to replace musicians who were not clique material—nothing unusual about that if the musician doesn't measure up, but this was done indiscriminately to some excellent musicians.

On a later band I was a benign member of the band's clique, but at least our machinations consisted of suggesting replacements for departing members. Only once did I toy with using my influence when a baritone man was unfailingly rude to me for no reason. I conquered the temptation to suggest that he be replaced.

The clique in Thornhill's band made it clear that they had no use for Iggy, so because I was married to him, I was always uneasy around them. On the bus they would make sly, sex-oriented remarks to me out of Iggy's hearing, and instead of telling them to knock it off (as I would today) I would laugh nervously, which only encouraged more of the same. I didn't dare tell Iggy because he had an ungovernable temper and I was afraid of what he might do. In fact, during an engagement at the old Pennsylvania Hotel someone in the band room made a remark Iggy didn't like and he pushed the offender's head into the toilet and started flushing it. He had to be restrained.

Although some band members not in the clique would often ask me to tell Claude that I had been asked to sing one of the arrangements made for me simply because they liked the way I sang it, I never relaxed enough with the band to sing them with any joy or confidence. I was convinced that the clique and Claude didn't like my singing, so I tried to tailor my style to fit what I thought they would like, with the result that neither they, nor I, were satisfied.

Claude's manager, Leonard Vannerson, was a wonderfully understanding man. He was married to Martha Tilton at the time and had had a great deal of at-home training in coping with the girl singer's sometimes baffling psyche. Just before a week-long engagement at the Steel Pier in Atlantic City, New Jersey, he told me that the clique was lobbying Claude to replace me with the sister of a former member of the band. To this end, they were taping the air checks from the Steel Pier and would use them as ammunition against me. If they were lucky and I was bad, they would play the tapes for Claude and I would be out. Leonard suggested that I watch my step on the broadcasts. I was so enraged and hurt by this that I demanded to leave the band that very day. I do not tolerate being placed on probation for any reason, and trying to sing well knowing my job depended on it was dehumanizing. Leonard had a similar experience when he managed Benny Goodman during the time Martha was singing with the band. He learned that she was being put on probation and when he told her about it she also demanded to get off the band immediately. Leonard got her off and he did the same for me.

I went to Atlantic City to visit Iggy who was still on the band. Leonard met me at the front door of the ballroom and said that when I heard my replacement sing I would find it hard to understand their objection to me. She was not a good singer but she was perfect clique material.

The clique soon turned their attention to my husband. They talked Claude into rehiring their old bass player, in addition to Iggy. This bass player hadn't been playing due to some emotional problems. The trouble was that he was still having them on the bandstand. It was humiliating for Iggy to stand side by side with another bass player who was clearly not capable of playing his bass. It was the perfect ploy to get rid of Iggy.

• 6 •

Alvino Rey

When Iggy joined Alvino Rey's band in Texas, I went back to California to live with my parents. But then Alvino's girl singer fell ill. As the contract read "seventeen men and a girl singer," the manager didn't want to take any chances of being canceled for breach of contract, so a search was on for a temporary replacement. Naturally Iggy told Alvino about me. I was so disillusioned from my bad experiences both on Georgie Auld's and, more recently, Claude Thornhill's bands that I said an emphatic "No." However, my mother urged me to take the job as it was only temporary—it was thus an opportunity for me to stretch out and sing exactly the way I wanted to because there was no question of my being fired. The idea made a lot of sense so I left for Texas.

I don't know what happened to the former girl singer on the band; I only know that there was never any mention of my leaving after what I thought would be a couple of weeks as a substitute.

Jimmy Joyce was the boy singer on the band, and he, the three trumpet players, and I made up the vocal group called the Blue Reys. Although the trumpet section stayed much the same, if a new trumpet player was hired he was required to sing in the vocal group. I have always liked group singing and thoroughly enjoyed singing the lead part. From time to time the group would be so inspired that we actually rehearsed on the bus, à la "Orchestra Wives." Alvino was with Capitol Records when Johnny Mercer was still one of the owners. The band was thrilled to be asked to record with Johnny, especially since the Blue Reys would be singing with him. Johnny had written special lyrics to "Glow Worm." At rehearsal we discovered that there was a final chorus missing. Johnny excused himself, saying he had to go to his office to get the lyrics. He was back in about fifteen minutes. He'd been *writing* the last chorus!

After a few months on the band Iggy felt that he was stagnating. He wanted to work with a band more jazz-oriented than Alvino's, so he left and joined Charlie Barnet.

Alvino always rehearsed at Art Whiting's studio on Santa Monica Boulevard when we were in town. Various arrangers who were struggling to get their work heard would sometimes bring in arrangements, and the band would run them down. One sad story concerns two arrangements brought in by two different arrangers on the same rehearsal day. The arrangements were both first rate, and Alvino either bought them or they were given to him. One of the arrangers that day was Nelson Riddle who went on to fame and fortune by writing for Nat Cole, Frank Sinatra, and Peggy Lee, as well as many successful television series. The other, though equally talented, wasn't so lucky; he ultimately committed suicide so that his wife and family could have his insurance.

When we were in town and not working, Iggy would go to the Whiting studio almost nightly to jam with some other musicians. He and I were barely civil to each other by then, but neither of us made a move to separate. One night a girlfriend and I drove him to Whiting's, and instead of dropping him off as was my custom, I decided to go in. I had never met with such resistance, both from Iggy and the drummer who had to unlock the door to the studio for us. I forged ahead anyway, and when I got into the studio I saw an attractive lady sitting at the piano, along with four other musicians, all of whom looked so stricken that I instantly understood what (or who) Iggy's nightly jam sessions included. It was the answer to a silent prayer. I had had the arrogant notion that if I asked for a divorce he'd be devastated, so this revelation came as a distinct relief.

Alvino's band was leaving for nine months on the road, so I suggested to Iggy that he apply for the divorce on the grounds that I had deserted him. He promised to do so.

There is positively nothing like an extended tour on the road—traveling in all kinds of weather, alternating freezing and sweltering, playing in ballrooms with miserable sound systems and pianos hopelessly out of tune, which gave the band members a big problem in tuning up. There were times when the pianist was forced to transpose up or down to get close to the band's tuning.

We played many outdoor gigs where a quick intake of breath before my next phrase often included a moth. Sitting under the bright lights which attracted a variety of large bugs was horrifying to me, but my reaction seemed to really amuse the band. I would be wearing a strapless gown, and dozens of times during the evening I would jump up screaming, shaking the collection of bugs off my bare shoulders, out of my lap, my hair, and worse, out of the bodice of my gown.

I was fortunate that I didn't bleach my hair because God knows what beauty salons on the road would have done to me. I can't remember the number of home permanents I gave myself at three o'clock in the morning in my hotel room after the job.

Applying makeup and dressing for the gig in the ballroom ladies' room with as many as fifteen curious customers' faces peering at me, observing my every movement, became routine. As a result of my aplomb at such moments Conte Candoli, the trumpet player on Ventura's band which I was later to join, tried to rattle me by standing inches from me as I applied makeup. I was undaunted!

I learned to sing (or croak) when I had laryngitis, an occupational hazard sometimes brought on by our inability to check into a hotel for several nights due to the inspired itinerary devised by our booking agency. It sometimes accepted dates for the band so many hundreds of miles apart there was barely enough time to make the gig, much less check into a hotel. I learned to sing despite total exhaustion. In short, I learned to sing.

Some of the bookings on our tour were crippling, especially the "one day theaters." This would be a series of about ten days in duration, another period in which the band never checked into a hotel but simply arrived at the theater each morning. We would jump off the bus, rehearse the acts previously booked by the theater, change into wardrobe, do three or four shows during the day and evening, change back into traveling clothes, jump back on the bus, and ride all night in order to arrive at the next theater for the routine to begin all over again. It's not easy under those conditions to be (reasonably) glamorous, well pressed, rested, in excellent voice—and civil.

Bands generally have two managers. One oversees the band in town, planning its future bookings, recordings, etc. The other manager is the road manager, and as his title implies, he travels with us and manages the road tour. Our road manager was Bill Young, a Canadian gentleman in every sense of the word. I can still hear Bill saying to the band after the evening's gig, "Bags at 8:30, leave at 9:00," accompanied by a series of groans from the band because bedtime was never before two or three a.m. There were always a few stragglers or oversleepers who, upon being awakened in the morning, rushed down looking bewildered, having had no time for breakfast or coffee. Departure time was inflexible because we usually had just enough time to get to the next engagement.

On the bus, Bill sat in the front seat just inside the door. I sat in the seat directly behind him, the dreaded seat that has the large bump by the window which accommodates one of the bus wheels. The window seat was so uncomfortable for two that I was granted sole occupancy.

Bill performed a gentlemanly service for me that no manager has ever performed before or since. When the bus pulled up in front of the hotel, he was the first one out. He would go into the hotel, check me in, and return holding my room key. He spoke beautifully and was a very elegant man, always dapper no matter the time. He always smoked using a cigarette holder, which made him look even more distinguished. He had a puckish wit and was a joy to be around. He used the word "begonia" when he referred to a part or thing that no gentleman of his stripe would call by its rightful name.

Bill seemed to feel that the band called for entirely too many rest stops and sometimes refused to stop. He was undoubtedly concerned that with such a long trip before us too many rest stops might make us late for the gig, and it was his responsibility to be sure that we arrived on time. However, if I asked for a rest stop, he didn't hesitate. Quite often a desperate band member would beg me to request a rest stop, knowing that for me Bill would stop.

On most bands there are the guys who drink and the guys who "turn on," or smoke marijuana. On Alvino's band the guys who turned on sat in the back section of the bus. They hung items of clothing between their group and the rest of us. It was like two separate bands. It took weeks for me to realize that when the bus suddenly smelled as if something were burning I was not to blurt this out because it jeopardized the "happy hour" in the back of the bus. I was none too popular until I worked this out.

Then there is the musician who hangs around the leader all the time. He is an object of scorn by the rest of the band. In fact, any kind of phony behavior is almost instantly recognized by the band members. When a new man is hired, by the time he takes that long walk to his chair on the stand, unpacks his horn, and plays a few preparatory notes, the band usually has his number. When I first joined the territory band in Nebraska, they made my life hell by playing in unison "The worms crawl in, the worms crawl out" for every step I took from the door to the bandstand.

There is something I have speculated about for years which is worth mentioning. When I first started singing with bands in the forties, the percentage of jazz musicians who were gay seemed to be zero. Today all that has changed. There are any number of famous musicians who are openly gay. They mostly are arrangers, singers, and musicians who don't usually travel with bands but have their own groups. There are so few traveling bands these days that it's difficult to estimate the percentage, but I'd be willing to bet that the players in bands are still heterosexual. There's still far too much resentment against gays, though there shouldn't be any.

When I was still working in bands I did a bit of research on this subject. The answers were sometimes silly, ranging from "Women are so soft and smell so nice," to my own opinion, which is that the budding musician spends most of his adolescent years practicing his instrument so, if he is serious, he has little time for chicks. Then he goes on the road with a band, and twelve chicks are hanging over the bandstand, clamoring for attention. I asked my good friend, the late Shelly Manne, whom I've known since 1941, how he felt about this theory of mine. He thought for a couple of minutes, shuddered and said, "What would the cats in the band say?" There were unconfirmed rumors about a couple of musicians being gay back then, but the ridicule and ostracism they would have had to endure had they admitted it kept them quiet. In the bands I've sung on, the musicians were a macho group whose sexual exploits were common knowledge on the bus.

The failure rate of marriages involving girl singers is staggering. Of the top girl singers in the country, few are presently married. Oh, they've all been married a few times but their marriages don't last. If the husband happens to be less successful than his wife, he resents being Mister Famous Girl Singer. All too often the husband is addressed by his wife's last name rather than his own.

The constant traveling takes its toll, of course. A feeling of absolute trust is essential to any marriage, but when the glamorous girl singer/wife is on the road and the husband is stuck at home, it is difficult to achieve. And certainly the reverse is true. Opportunities abound on the road, and what may seem like a harmless diversion can have dire consequences. I can personally recollect at least three marriages that went on the rocks when hubby brought home an unwelcome present. Today there is multiple choice disease, while back then it was gonorrhea or syphilis. (God knows how much gonorrhea was explained away as being simple "strain.")

Alvino's regular manager was not a particular fan of mine, although he was always pleasant. I had one encounter with him that must have taken a lot out of him. He was having a struggle trying to convince me that I should wear falsies. He began by saying that the King Sisters had been known to wear them to make their gowns look more glamorous, and he cited several other examples of ladies who wore them. At the end of this speech which was obviously quite embarrassing to him, I said, "But you don't understand. I *am* wearing falsies." This seemed to bring our conversation to an end. (I once asked my good friend, jazz critic Ralph J. Gleason, why I never made the front page of *Downbeat*, only the inside pages. He deadpanned, "No tits.")

The manager also found it troubling that I displayed a zany sense of humor off the bandstand but didn't show my audience what a sparkling personality I possessed. He asked one of the arrangers to write a piece that would show me off. I loved the new arrangement, but I still didn't do a lot of dancing on the bandstand.

If you were to add up all the four hours a night spent sitting on the bandstand during a gig, the total would be staggering—and boring. There were always a few traditional girl singer things you could do in order to look lively. Something that used to irritate me was the customer who danced up and said, "Whatsa matter, honey, did somebody die? Can't you smile once in a while?" Meanwhile, the muscles around my mouth were aching from all of the foolish grinning I had been doing all night. Then there were the little left forefinger to right crooked elbow, then right finger to left crooked elbow, gestures done in time to the music, and of course, there was clapping on two and four. (One and three? Unthinkable!)

It was customary for the girl singer to sit stage right of the band between the sax section and the piano. Invariably the leader would call out the next tune, and the pianist would be unable to hear it. Often the arrangement would start with an eight-bar piano solo. I would jump up, find his music, tell him the key, and lay out his part. He could always get through the first eight bars if I told him the song and the key. I'm sure I didn't endear myself to the baritone player when in order to hone my reading skills I softly sang his part along with him.

One bitter winter night we were working somewhere in Minnesota in a converted barn. (I was not aware of any extensive conversion.) The band grouped around a pot-bellied stove for its sole and meager warmth. I accessorized my gown by wearing mittens. The only lighting for the stage was one light in a socket against the back wall. When Alvino played "Stormy Weather," he did it with sound effects on his steel guitar, somehow producing sounds of thunder and other appropriate inclement weather noises. One night during the rendition of this number and at the place where Alvino was accustomed to making his weather sounds, one of the trombone players reached up and pulled the switch to the light several times, simulating lightning. Instant collapse into laughter from the band. Despite the hardships, the camaraderie or mutual misery always produced some truly funny moments.

We were working in the Town Casino in Buffalo, New York, and the club employed a line of lovely chorus girls. The stage had stairways on both sides which led up to a stage above the band's heads. Back of that stage, which was curtained, were the casts' dressing rooms. I was a little frightened of the girls in the chorus, but eventually they befriended me. One night, unbeknownst to the band, they dressed me up. I applied stage makeup and donned a short ruffled satin one-shoulder dress and fishnet stockings. One of the acts that the band accompanied did an Apache dance. Apache is a word for a Parisian ruffian or gangster, and this dance was a rather violent one, performed customarily by a man and a woman. In this act, the man appeared to toss the woman around the stage, but it was all carefully choreographed to look more violent than it actually was.

When the upstairs curtain rose, I was leaning against a lamp post, cigarette in holder dangling carelessly out of my mouth. I say carelessly, because I have never smoked and looked really gauche when I pretended to. When the band caught sight of me, they were unable to play the opening bars—they were much too busy laughing. The laughter escalated during the act, because what I didn't know was that the dancers and chorus line decided I should be a part of this dance but they failed to notify me. I found myself being thrown around the stage, and although I was never hurt, the amazement on my face kept the band and the audience laughing throughout the act.

The comic on the show with us at the Town Casino was Jack E. Leonard. I have always been very partial to comics and am accustomed to the way they use the band as the butt of many of their jokes. However, Jack went a bit too far with his jokes about the band, some of them being downright cruel. They got even in a big way! They changed the key signatures on some of his arrangements and added unnecessary flats and sharps to the rest. I can just imagine the new band's confusion on the next Jack E. Leonard engagement! Childish, but fun.

A few of the musicians' wives were pretty bitchy toward me, and I never could understand it. Was the bitchiness a form of jealousy because I could travel all year long on the bus with their husbands? One of the musicians told me he had a compliment for me from a group of the wives who were sitting out front listening to the band. They told him they found it positively amazing that I still looked so good after the life I led. (I was twenty-seven!) It was definitely not a compliment, but the musician was completely oblivious to this.

We arrived early one day in some town in Ohio, and before the gig that night two of the saxophonists got busted. (They were part of the back of the bus group.) It was on the local news every thirty minutes all day long, so that night we had a considerable crowd. They'd come to see the addicts, I expect. We all purposely twitched every now and then to make it worth the price of their admission.

We were hired for a graduation dance in Corvallis, Oregon. The manager based in Los Angeles occasionally joined the band on the road when the road manager, Bill Young, took a few days off. He had had difficulty in getting sleeping accommodations at the motel for us because the few bands they had put up before were so destructive. However, one of the society bands had come through a few weeks prior to our arrival and had been perfect gentlemen. So, with a lot of urging on the manager's part and promises that we were an orderly and well-behaved band, they reluctantly decided to let us stay.

When we left the Corvallis motel that had been so hesitant about providing rooms for us, we were secure in the knowledge that we had been exemplary guests. We drove several hundred miles toward the next job and stopped at a gas station a few miles before reaching town to ask directions. We saw a police car at the station but thought nothing of it. The manager got off the bus and had a brief conversation with the police, after which he stomped back on the bus in a towering rage. He announced that the police were there because they had had a call from the motel manager in Corvallis saying that two of their blankets were missing. The motel manager had asked the police to stop the bus and arrest the thief. Our manager said, "All right, who stole the blankets from the motel?" Silence. Finally the guilty sax player spoke up mildly. He said, "Man, I didn't steal the blankets. I borrowed them so I could sleep on the bus during the next few one-nighters. Then I was gonna send them back." The manager was apoplectic and screamed, "Borrow, my ass. You stole those blankets!" He stormed off the bus with the offending blankets. In the silence, the baritone saxophonist sitting next to the sax player said quietly, "If it's cool in your mind, man, it's cool." Lovely.

The band wore tuxes that night, in order to match the formally dressed graduates in the audience. One of our saxophone players who sat behind the improvised curtain on the bus was a brilliant player but somewhat—how shall I put it?—different. He was playing a perfectly beautiful chorus, standing out in front of the band at the mike, when the band happened to look at the saxophonist's feet and began to laugh. He was wearing galoshes.

The closing routine of the night always began with Johnny Mercer's "Dream" as part of a medley that ended with "Goodnight Sweetheart." Alvino sat at his steel guitar out front, playing the melody. (The band called his instrument the "sewing machine.") All of a sudden there was a series of squeaks and clicking sounds. Our "different" sax player was getting a head start by taking apart all of his instruments, first blowing the saliva out, then packing them up one by one, snapping the cases shut sharply all the while we were playing. Jimmy Joyce and I were never any help because we always laughed at everything. I was looking through some old pictures taken of us sitting on various bandstands around the country, and there wasn't one where we weren't busily discussing something, rather than paying attention to the audience.

The next few days the band's schedule left us very little time for sleeping in our hotel rooms along the way, so our sax player decided to save money and sleep on the bus.

Rocky Cole was hired to play piano, but since he was not yet a member of the local musician's union, he was unable to play for the first few weeks until he could get his card. He sat in front with Jimmy and me and sang a few novelty tunes.

Occasionally Alvino would introduce Jimmy Joyce by saying he was a Marine war veteran who had fought valiantly for our country.

(This was true.) One night Rocky turned to Jimmy after this introduction and said, "Man, you couldn't even fight your way out of a paper bag," whereupon Jimmy drew himself up to his full five foot five and said defensively, "I could too!"

Other nights Alvino would introduce Jimmy by identifying him as Marine Sergeant James Joyce, First Marine Battalion, such and such company and such and such platoon. As many service men know from their travels around the country, there's usually a little old lady who, upon seeing the uniform, asks if you know her grandson. I grew so used to this introduction I hardly listened anymore. One night as a joke I asked Jimmy if by chance he knew my cousin, Ronald Burroughs, also a Marine. He looked at me strangely. I couldn't figure out why. It turned out that my cousin was his best friend when they served on Guadalcanal together. Naturally the next time the band played near Camp Pendleton in San Diego where my cousin was stationed, the two of them had a grand reunion. So folks, don't ignore those little old ladies—the chances are you *do* know their grandsons.

The Air Force had an arrangement with various name bands whereby they would fly the band to a one-nighter. In exchange for this free ride we would play dance jobs at the base. The airplanes used to transport us were not designed for comfort, nor did they inspire great confidence. They had once been olive drab but were sadly in need of a fresh paint job. We sat on bucket seats. The aisles were piled high with the band's instruments and equipment. We were all issued parachutes and given a brief demonstration of what to do if we had to use them. These briefings only added to our discomfiture. I traveled in skirts, finding them much more comfortable than trousers, so I was a strange sight indeed, with the straps of the parachute fastening under my crotch, exposing two white triangles of gleaming flesh for all the world to see.

Alvino chartered a plane to take us back to Los Angeles from Arizona. We had barely taken off when I casually peered through the window and saw the engine was on fire. Nobody panicked as we were over an Air Force field. The pilot asked permission to land. It was denied. He explained our predicament but got the same answer. We simply landed anyway. We were told to stay on or around the plane while it was being repaired. We did this . . . for eight hours!

After the tour was over, I returned to Los Angeles, working sporadically with Alvino. One day I got a call from a Chicago-based composer/musician/friend. He was in town and asked if I'd ever seen the movie *Hamlet* with Olivier. I hadn't, so he invited me to see it with him. I remember we sat in the balcony and I was enthralled by the superb acting and the marvelous score by William Walton. My friend had seen the movie a dozen times so he simply sat and enjoyed my reaction to the movie.

My rapt attention must have convinced him that inside my fluffy blonde head may lurk a mind, so one evening he took the bus to my home and read some very obscure poetry to my mother and me for an entire evening. It was rough going some of the time but we survived. When it was time for him to leave, it was pouring rain, so my mother offered to drive him back to his hotel. My father was out that evening and had driven our "good" car, so we took his Model A Ford. My father had given up baking and become a journeyman electrician. He had bought this car specifically for driving to work. It had a perfect engine but looked absolutely disgraceful. The black paint had rusted, the roof leaked though my father had poured some tar over the roof in an effort to prevent the leaking. (It didn't.) The tar had run down and dried on all the windows in sticky rivulets. In addition, there were no floorboards, so as you tooled along you could also watch the pavement go by beneath your feet. We left our apartment, carrying the umbrella. The musician was appalled when he saw the car, but gamely got in back with me. When I raised the umbrella in the car he almost lost his nerve, but when he saw the street passing under his feet he came undone. I'm sure he never forgot that harrowing ride, but he certainly forgot me, because I never heard from him again.

Earlier in this book I spoke of the girl singer's inclination to find a kindred spirit on the band, and I found one on Alvino's.

It all began quite innocently while we were on the long nine-month tour of the country. This man had been on the band for some time, and we were good friends. He played trumpet which meant he also sang with the Blue Reys singing group. He did some arranging for the band and occasionally accompanied Alvino on his flights to the next engagement. He knew that I was separated from Iggy. He also felt that, as I had a couple of years invested in the marriage, perhaps I shouldn't give it up so hastily. Something about "better to dance with the devil you know…." He had been married for many years to an attractive woman who also lived in California, but in another city. We were thrown together through the singing group and slowly discovered that our friendship had turned into love. It became obvious to the band that we were the new twosome and they seemed to accept it.

The romance went on for some months, but after much soul searching he decided that his wife needed him more than I did. I vowed never to allow myself to become deeply involved with a married man again and to that end made some stringent rules:

1. Perhaps you can call me if I don't know your wife.
2. Don't call me if your wife is in the same town as we are unless you're willing to meet me at least five hundred miles from home.
3. Probably not if your wife is an acquaintance of mine.
4. Certainly not if she is!

Although these rules were made as kind of a joke, I have never broken any of them. The breakup was painful enough to teach me a lesson about married men.

The band manager began to hint, then threaten, to replace me with the youngest King sister, Marilyn. After a while it got to be too much and I quit the band.

I owe a great deal to Alvino, who had great faith in my ability. He acted as buffer between the manager and me and never interfered with my vocal experimentation. By the time I left the band I had developed a singing style.

• 7 •

San Francisco and the Stan Kenton All-Stars

Recently a girl singer friend of mine was bemoaning the fact that at age twenty-seven she was still living at home between gigs. It set me to thinking that I lived at home or on the road until I married André Previn. I don't recall ever paying or even offering to pay rent at home. I also don't recall my parents ever complaining. It never even occurred to me to get a place of my own. I was just very lucky to have the kind of parents I had.

I had been home a couple of weeks when I decided to drive to San Francisco to visit some relatives. Iggy had told me about a bass player in San Francisco named Vernon Alley and suggested I look him up. One night I went into Facks (the first one on Market Street) and introduced myself, and Vernon asked me to sing a couple of tunes. A few days later Vernon called and said the owner had given them a raise, and they had agreed to add a small portion of their salaries to it in the hopes that I'd come up and sing with the group. I was only too happy to oblige.

Vernon was using a quartet: piano, bass, drums, and alto sax. Pony Poindexter was the saxophonist, and he and the pianist, Richard Wyands, went on to become famous in the jazz world. We had a great time working together except when the owner came in. The room was very long, and the bar ran almost the entire length of the club. The owner would walk in, see how sparse the crowd was, clap his hands to his head, and moan aloud. It made us wonder if we'd been wise to give up our day jobs. The owner's brother was the bartender, and when not actively mixing drinks he stood at the end of the bar directly across from the band, no more than six feet away. It seemed that, every time I sang a ballad, he and a customer would play a dice game which consisted of the two shaking the dice in a cup and slamming it down on the bar. The other trial for any entertainer is when the bartender blends drinks. I've noticed now the new cash registers make a terrible racket while toting up the check. Certainly any of these options were better than the night a fist fight broke out right in front of the band. I happened to be singing and I sang on until the end. By then the fight was over. I said, "Is there any other tune you'd particularly like to fight to?"

My parents came in to town and brought my uncle and aunt into the club to hear me. My aunt was Canadian and did a high wire act in the circus in her youth. She was a dear lady, but I often had trouble keeping a straight face because of her many malaprops. She topped herself in Facks that night. She stared at Vernon Alley for a very long time, then said, "Don't I know you from somewhere?" Vernon said, "I don't think so." After another bout of staring she suddenly said, "Weren't you with Lyle Hamilton's band?" Vernon said he hadn't been. After a moment he said, "You don't mean Lionel Hampton, do you?" (He'd been with that band.) My aunt brightened, turned to my uncle, and said, "See, didn't I tell you he was with Lyle Hamilton." Poor Lionel, he's been Lyle Hamilton from that day to this.

The Mohawk carpet company had a fifteen-minute show in the fall with Roberta Quinn as the singer. They were looking for a summer replacement and I was offered the job. I hired a terrific piano player named Buddy Matzinger. The set consisted of a grand piano! If I moved a foot away from its edges, I was out of the picture, so as I sang I inched my way around the piano until I landed in the curve. We began the show with me standing to Buddy's left. Our opening was the song "Get Happy." We just did the first eight bars of the tune, "Forget your troubles and just get happy, forget your troubles and all be gay, forget your troubles and just get happy, get ready for the show today." I am embarrassed every time I think of the last line, which was my idea. I would then say, "Hi, Buddy." Buddy would say, "Hi, Betty," and we'd get on with the show. Ever since that summer, wherever I see Buddy, we go through the entire opening of that little show.

It was a wonderful opportunity for us to do whatever tune we fancied, including the verse to any tune that had one. I could sit on the piano bench if I didn't know the verse and read it, then stand up for the chorus, which I usually knew. I was also working at Facks at night.

When the summer ended, I went back to Los Angeles. Stan Kenton had disbanded his big band temporarily, and I got a call from one of his former sidemen asking me if I'd like to sing with an all-star group made up of Kenton alumni. They were: Milt Bernhardt on trombone; Art Pepper on alto; Bob Cooper on tenor sax; Don Bagley on bass; Fred Otis on piano; and Jimmy Pratt on drums. The band was booked by General Artists Corporation (GAC), and our first gig was in Los Angeles. The next one was in San Francisco on the Barbary Coast in a club that was presenting jazz for the first time. It was a strip joint with a comic/MC whose warmup was about as offensive as any I've heard. He opened with "The Vaseline Corporation of America Presents Up Your Ass." His act went steadily downhill from there.

The makeup of the show must have been confusing for the audience. It opened with our band playing a forty-five minute jazz set, then the MC's comedy act, followed by two or three strippers.

The band room and the strippers' dressing rooms were downstairs, and I shall never forget Bob Cooper's face as the strippers—completely nude, having just finished their show—came back downstairs, passing us on our way up to do our next show. What do I mean when I say I'll never forget Coop's face? I never saw it because as the strippers passed him he turned it to the wall!

We traveled in two cars. Coop drove his convertible with Fred Otis, Art Pepper, and me as passengers, and the rest of the group rode in the other car. We were booked into Rawlings, Wyoming, and the car in which I rode left town first. When we arrived in Sinclair, Wyoming, we called GAC in Los Angeles to ask the name of the club in Rawlings, only to find that the job had been canceled. The rest of the band had been notified, but they hadn't been able to catch us before we left.

So here we were in Sinclair, Wyoming, with no job and no money. We checked into the Sinclair Hotel and signed the tab for our meals and rooms for four days until GAC sent enough money to bail us out. We managed to have a good time despite our troubles, because every night we'd go downstairs to the ballroom to play and sing a few tunes to the unexpected delight of the hotel guests.

For some reason Stan Kenton could never recognize me when we met. He was constantly apologizing for his oversight. Little did he know that I harbored a certain amount of guilt about my own reaction the first time I heard his name. I was living in New York, and someone told me that Stan Kenton was looking for a girl singer. Stan's band was playing at Frank Dailey's Meadowbrook at that time. I had no idea who Stan Kenton was in those days, so when I spoke to him about coming out for the audition I asked him who would be playing piano for me. How was I to know that he was the piano player! In fact, since I had no idea who he was, I didn't bother to go out for the audition. Years later when the band was once again looking for a girl singer, they set about it by doing a weekly radio show in the form of a contest wherein several singers would appear and the best singer of that week would be chosen. This went on for a number of weeks. Each week the best of the new group would be picked, and the final week a winner would be selected from the weekly winners. About a week before the finals the manager of the band called and asked me if I'd appear as one of the winners on the final show. He assured me that I would win the contest and then join the band. (I don't know how this all ended, except that Chris Connor was the next singer. For all I know, they made her the same offer.) I asked the manager how they could get away with this as I had never appeared on any of the shows and the other singers would surely be aware of this. He seemed to feel that it would work out all right. In the end, I didn't do the show and never sang with the band except for the Stan Kenton All-Stars. I found it terribly disillusioning that this sort of thing could happen. I had a further shock a few years later when I was in the office of the manager of several artists, mostly singers. The office personnel was busily filling in their clients' names in hundreds of *Downbeat* magazines, thereby ensuring a win in their yearly poll. They looked up when I came in and said, "Too bad we already have a girl singer. Otherwise we'd fill in your name." I haven't attached too much importance to polls since then.

I have always had a great fondness for comics and, in fact, use humor in my show. But there is one comic for whom I had no fondness. Henry Morgan had a little television show in Los Angeles on one of the lesser-known and -watched television stations. On this particular show, the other guest was the fine actor, Everett Sloan. Someone had arranged for me to sing a tune on the show. I wore a low-cut red plaid wool dress from Jax, red pantyhose, and red shoes. Part of this wardrobe figured in my later humiliation. I sang the Gershwin tune "But Not for Me." The last note I sing in the arrangement is a bit unusual. Dizzy Gillespie called it "the flatted fifth." The moment my last note died out, Henry Morgan said, "You sang a wrong note!" I looked to my accompanist and asked if it was true. He seemed to shake his head yes. (Later he said he didn't even hear the question.) Morgan turned to the audience and said, "All right, those of you who think she sang a wrong note, raise your hand." A couple of people raised hands. "How many of you think she sang the right note?" Big show of hands and much applause. I stood there absolutely destroyed. Everett Sloan (who was a big jazz fan) jumped in and explained that I was a jazz singer and perhaps Henry Morgan just didn't understand what I was singing. Morgan turned to me and said, "I haven't embarrassed you, have I?" I pointed to my red pantyhose and said, "These may look like red stockings to you; they're actually blood!" (How can I respect the opinion of a man whose theme was "The Bear Came Over the Mountain"!)

Art Pepper raved about a young trumpet player with Charlie Ventura named Conte Candoli, saying he's the best white trumpet player in the world. The next time I worked in San Francisco, I sang at the Blackhawk. While there, someone told me that Jackie Cain and Roy Kral were leaving Ventura, and he was looking for a replacement. I decided to try out.

• 8 •

Charlie Ventura and Woody Herman

I met Charlie and his manager in their hotel room. There was no piano, so Charlie played guitar (badly) while I sang a couple of tunes. I was hired. They neglected to tell me that the manager's wife was also joining the band as a singer. Had I known, I might not have been so eager to accept the job as later circumstances were to prove. Although my girl singer friends claim there is no jealousy among them, there is a kind of friendly rivalry. As an example, recently I worked one night in a local club, and two excellent girl singers came in to hear me. After the set, which I thought went very well, one of the singers said, "That last tune you sang, I sing that too." The other singer said, "Well, how did *you* think you sounded?" God forbid they should pay me a compliment!

My first gig with the Ventura band was in Denver. Although from then on we traveled by private car, this time I was given an airplane ticket because I needed the extra time to learn a few of the arrangements most requested by the Ventura fans. Singing with Charlie's band wasn't just singing a few choruses of standard tunes; it involved singing bebop syllables in unison with the horns. Charlie gave me a couple of his records and found a local friend with an apartment containing a record player, and I spent the afternoon singing the tunes over and over, hoping something would stick.

Shortly before I joined the band, Miles Davis's wonderful album called "Miles Davis Tentette" was released. It included some stunning original tunes, and the arrangements were some of the best I have ever heard. In fact, nearly every tune on this album has become a jazz standard. I happened to own the album and knew most of the tunes.

It's a painfully lonely feeling, being new on a band, wanting to be liked and accepted. I had my opening at intermission while the band was raving about the Miles Davis album. They had just heard it but were unfamiliar with the tunes. I jumped in and sang a couple of them. They were pleasantly surprised.

In the old days the girl singer wasn't given much respect by the musicians—I think the situation has changed some since then. The only person given less respect than the girl singer was the boy singer, so perhaps the fact that I knew, and could sing, a few of the tunes from the hottest new Miles album set me apart from the band's usual perception of "the girl singer" as nothing more than a commercial gimmick.

Perhaps Charlie thought that using two singers singing unison parts with him would sound more like Jackie and Roy. Jackie Cain and Roy Kral were the original singers with Charlie's band. They were later married. Roy had written many of the vocal and instrumental arrangements for the band, in addition to a couple of originals, so he and Jackie had learned the lines together and from the beginning their syllables were identical. The manager's wife (whom I will never identify) had the advantage because she had been traveling with the band and had learned the syllables by listening to Jackie and Roy nightly. Singing the lines was not the problem; matching the unfamiliar syllables to the other singer was, and I had only one afternoon to attempt to meet the challenge. The manager's wife was helpful in the beginning, running over the syllables with me so that we sang the same ones. Later on, since I could read and she couldn't, I would teach her any new material that came in, and she and I would decide together what syllables to use.

After Art Pepper's glowing review of Conte Candoli's trumpet playing, I was looking forward to hearing him play. Charlie had an outstanding band at that time: Boots Musilli on alto; Benny Green on trombone; Conte on trumpet; and Ed Shaughnessy on drums. The pianist and bass player were replaced with Dave McKenna and Red Mitchell, shortly after I joined the band. Charlie, of course, played tenor and baritone, but I personally much preferred his baritone playing.

In a sense, this was the first real exposure I had had as a "jazz" singer. The bands I had sung with before (aside from Georgie Auld and Claude Thornhill) were certainly not "society bands," but they were not, as the slogan for Charlie's band stated, "The Band That Plays Bebop for the People." The audiences expected a great deal more from the other singer and me, especially as we had followed the popular Jackie and Roy.

When the band played Bop City, we worked opposite Count Basie. Jimmy Rushing was singing with the band at that time, and he would sit in the corner outside Basie's dressing room, seemingly asleep, but missing none of the drama. The band's dressing rooms were up one flight from Basie. Our band members lived at the Forest Hotel which was across the street from the backstage entrance and the stage door and was passionately defended by the guards. They came to know who we were and would let us pass without a hassle after we'd been there a few nights. One night I walked out the front door with some friends and stood talking to them for a few minutes. When I walked back to the front door, the guard turned me away. It was humbling, standing there trying to convince the guard that I sang with Charlie and had been working there for three weeks. I pointed to the picture of me out in front to no avail. In the end, I went to the backstage door.

When my dearest girlfriend came to New York City to visit me, she was such a beauty she caused quite a stir backstage. One evening she promised to meet Basie for a drink at the Theresa Hotel the next afternoon. She had no intention of meeting him, but didn't know how to say no gracefully. The next night she and I walked by the open door of his dressing room and without looking up, Basie said, "Some people just ain't got no word." Jimmy Rushing opened one eye and chuckled.

Basie was not my friend's only conquest. Charlie was very interested in her as well. This was the inadvertent cause of a change in the lineup of the band. Symphony Sid did a remote broadcast from Bop City every night, and I don't know if it was lack of interest or poor memory that caused him to introduce the manager's wife and me on the air as "the two young ladies," when both our names were short and simple. After Basie's set, just before we went on, our road manager, George Morte, would set out two chairs for the other singer and me. I didn't see the other singer but went out and sat in my chair anyway. Some time passed while I sat there alone. Finally George came out and took away the other chair, inexplicably. That was the last I saw of the other singer. One good thing came of it, however, because now I knew that Symphony Sid would be bound to announce me by name at last. It was not to be. That night he introduced me to the radio audience as "the young lady." (Rumor had it that the other singer confessed to our manager, her husband, that she had been having an affair with Charlie. When she saw his interest in my friend, she was so jealous she told her husband of the affair. I have no idea whether this was true.)

Our band played opposite Basie at Bop City in 1949, long before Joe Williams joined him. By now I was feeling a little more secure as a jazz singer and was beginning to get some recognition. One night Billie Holiday came in to hear the Basie band, and when they took an intermission she started to leave. Sweets Edison (one of the trumpet players on the band, along with Gerald Wilson, Clark Terry, and Shorty Baker) asked her to stick around to hear me sing. Happily he didn't mention it to me before the set because I would have panicked.

In fact, of the many famous musicians in Bop City that I was blissfully unaware of, one was Louis Armstrong. The Ventura band played a benefit at the Howard Theater in Washington, D.C., and I was primping in the dressing room when behind me I heard an unmistakable voice say, "You sho' knocked me out in Bop City." Of course it was Louis.

The Bop City gig was both terrifying and rewarding. Always before I had worked with big bands in large ballrooms containing indifferent sound systems and filled with hundreds of people who were there to dance, not listen to the girl singer. But this was the "big time." The fans who came into Bop City sat quietly and listened. There was no dancing, no dice games, and no fighting! I learned to cope with the kind of stress that produced.

One night Basie asked me if I would like to join his band. I asked him if he was eager for both of us to die, what with the social climate in those days. He explained that, although I couldn't work down south with them, I could do theaters and record dates and clubs up north. I was too chicken to do it. After Joe Williams came along and eclipsed all the other singers, I asked Basie if I could change my mind and join the band. He laughed and told me it was too late. How I wish I had had the courage to take him up on his offer.

Conte, Benny Green, and I rode in the car George Morte drove. I used to take a terrible risk and carry whatever grass certain members of the band possessed. I didn't smoke grass myself, and I suppose I thought if I got caught I could convince the cops of my innocence. One day we were driving out of Chicago en route to pick up Benny Green on the South Side. I was knitting something at the time, and someone in the car was rolling a joint. As we drove up to where we were to meet Benny, we could see him, along with the friend who had driven him there, being shaken down by two cops.

Quick as a flash I grabbed the joints and stuffed them into my bra. I put the remaining stash in my knitting bag. I have to think that the shakedown was racial in nature because when the white cops didn't find anything on Benny and his friend they didn't make any attempt to shake the rest of us down—and a good thing, too.

Riding in the car on the way to a gig, Benny Green told Conte and me that we were wasting a lot of money. Every night we paid for two rooms, but only used one. He said he and Sarah Vaughan had been on Billy Eckstine's band together, and when they became an item they only rented one room. By now Conte and I were also an "item," so we decided to take his advice. This was a first for me, and I well remember the sinking feeling I had as Conte registered us as "Mr. and Mrs." It got a lot easier.

I don't know what the usual arrangement is when an unmarried couple is traveling on the road, but mine was that I paid for my meals and half the hotel room. It seemed to me to be very unfair to Conte to be expected to pay for everything because I was his lady. On our rare nights out it was different. It was a date and he paid.

Later on when I was with Benny Goodman, whose band was about one-fourth black, we had the heartbreaking chore of dropping the black musicians off in the black neighborhood, then driving on to the white hotels where the rest of the band stayed. With Charlie, there was only one black, Benny Green. We had reserved several studio apartments in Chicago and when we arrived and the apartment manager saw Benny and told him they were all booked up, Conte and I were so outraged we refused to stay. Instead, we went to a hotel.

The band played a week in Milwaukee at the Drum Lounge. One night after the job I was in the bathroom taking care of some matters of a personal nature when I happened to look up at the transom. There was a face looking back at me. I've never had a more sickening feeling. I ran out of the bathroom and told Conte, who rushed out into the hall in pursuit of the man. Although he didn't catch him, he was able to see the flash of a red jacket as it disappeared into the stairwell. He reported this episode to the desk, and the next morning the manager told us it had been one of the bellmen and he had been fired.

Later that day the bellman called me and said that he was a married man with three small children and was working at the hotel in order to put himself through college. He couldn't explain what had come over him to do such a thing, he'd never done it before, etc. He said he was calling because he had not told his wife, and if we were going to call the police, he'd rather be the one to tell her. In the end, I felt guiltier than he did.

From time to time Charlie would call us all down to the band room of whatever club we were appearing in and deliver a lecture. I was never quite clear as to what he meant to convey, but it seemed to have something to do with the fact that the soloists who preceded him took too many choruses, and by the time his solo came, he felt like the cleanup man. He would pace back and forth in front of us, getting more and more furious. At the end of one of these diatribes he said, "Now go back out there and I want to see a happy band!" After this attack, we looked at each other in wonderment. What had he left us to be happy about?

There's something that has always seemed terribly unfair about the uneven reception given the various musicians on the band. For instance, the drum solo always breaks an audience up. Benny Green, God bless him, always broke it up with his single line shifting of the time. Boots Musilli was a facile player, and that in itself is always a terrific crowd pleaser. Then came Conte, an understated, inventive, melodic, harmonic soloist whose playing went over the heads of most of the audiences. For him the applause was restrained. I've seen him be very depressed over the lack of appreciation for what he was playing. I have to put it down to the fact that most of the audience knows so little about jazz it responds to players who, to put it simply, play very fast or very loud. Happily, today Conte gets standing ovations.

Then the accent seemed to be on facility rather than invention. Nothing has changed. I don't mean that I have no admiration for those musicians who have amazing control of their horns, but they are inclined to play such torrents of notes I often feel that I'd give a fortune for an occasional quarter note. Very few people play and leave "spaces" anymore. Besides that, sometimes I don't want to listen that fast!

Why is it that when the tenor player honks or squeaks up above his horn's capacity I want to suggest that he play a horn that plays in that register, like, say, an alto. In my opinion the best examples of creative, tasteful, swinging, and soulful tenor players are Stan Getz, Zoot Sims, and Al Cohn. Early on they all listened to Lester Young and went on from there. They are all gone now, but thank God they left a lot of recordings behind.

The band spent two months in New York City during the steamiest part of the year, working first in Bop City, then at the Apollo Theater in Harlem. Conte and I were movie freaks, and it was just as well because the temperature was over a hundred degrees and the theaters, unlike our hotel room, were air-conditioned. We would arise at noon, have breakfast, and go to a movie; have a snack and go to a movie; have dinner and go on to a club. One night we went to the Three Deuces on 52nd Street. Passing the bar on the right and against the wall on the left was one long bench attached to the wall that ran the length of the club. The tables were placed in front of this bench. I was sitting alone in the corner at the extreme end of this bench one night while Conte went to the bar to say hello to a friend. Presently a couple of men brought a semi-comatose man and sat him down beside me. His head promptly fell on my shoulder. Shortly after, Conte came over and asked me if I'd like to meet Bud Powell. He was a legend to me, and I was delighted to meet him so I said yes. Conte said, "That's him. He's sleeping on your shoulder."

Later, when we were working in Philadelphia, we heard Bud was working at the Clique Club, and we decided to go hear him. The club is built on two levels. The bandstand serves as the separation between the two levels. We were sitting on the street level when from the room above appeared four men carrying a man completely out of it. I asked Conte who the man was. Once again it was Bud Powell. So, I've never met Bud Powell!

After the job at night we always went somewhere to eat. When I think of the mounds of exotic food we used to consume just before retiring I wonder how any of us lived through it. And why did we eat in so many Chinese and Italian restaurants to say nothing of rib joints. Were they the only restaurants that stayed open late enough to accommodate us?

I was often asked what time I went to bed after having worked until two a.m. When I said it was usually around five or six in the morning, my questioners would be amazed. I had to remind them that when they got off work at five in the afternoon they certainly didn't go right home to bed, so my hours were really not that unlike theirs.

Later, when I was married to André, who in those days had never traveled on the road, we spent the occasional weekend in Palm Springs, and one morning we overslept and missed breakfast. Although it was noon, we wanted some eggs. I looked up and down the street and from years of experience on the road, pointed out a likely place in which to have breakfast. Sure enough, the menu featured breakfast served all day. To prove a point, we saw Georgie Auld and another musician having breakfast. André couldn't understand how I knew just where to go.

Despite some of the irritations about Charlie's band, I would have to say that singing with the band was musically rewarding. Singing with a regular big band, the girl singer is lucky if she sings two tunes per set. At least with Charlie I not only sang my two standards, I also used my voice as an instrument and in each set sang several of the tunes with the band. Conte and I also did a couple of the Charlie Parker tunes, using syllables.

We were rehearsing at Bop City one day when Ventura called Conte a phony. Anyone who knows Conte knows how preposterous this is. I quit the band that same afternoon. After many promises and much urging I reluctantly agreed to come back. Conte left Charlie to go with Woody Herman's band. I stayed on. Charlie's brother, a good trumpet player, took Conte's place. Although he played the parts as written, I had no idea how much Conte had added to the arrangements. We dragged on for a few more weeks until Charlie broke up the band.

Woody's band was hired to play at the Tropicana in Havana. This was 1950. Conte took me with him. That was some band! Shelly Manne, Milt Jackson, Ralph Burns, Red Mitchell, Conte, Bill Harris, and Dave Barbour, Peggy Lee's former husband.

The Tropicana was some distance out of Havana, and we made arrangements with cab drivers to drive us out and back every night. The showroom/dance floor/bandstand was outdoors and it rained almost every night for a short period, leaving the floor wet. Dave Barbour was afraid if he plugged in his guitar he'd be electrocuted instantly. He may as well have stayed at home as we could barely hear him.

Some of us lived in a hotel in Havana, but Red Mitchell and Milt Jackson shared a flea-bitten apartment on the outskirts on the way to the Tropicana so they could do their own cooking. Most of the time they were fighting cockroaches, but we did have a good meal at their apartment one night. (Chicken, not cockroaches.)

After the job, our carload, which consisted of Bill Harris, Conte, and me, would stop at an outdoor beer parlor halfway back to Havana where we would have a few drinks. My problem was I wasn't much of a drinker and only wanted to get back to the hotel. To this end I learned a phrase in Spanish which I delivered to the cab driver who only barely spoke or understood English. I said, "Regreseramos ahora para la Habana," which roughly translated means "We will go back now to Havana." Maybe it was my accent, but nobody paid the slightest attention to my request!

We were there during Bautista's reign and the unrest was palpable. One night on the way home from the Tropicana, out on the open, dark, and deserted highway, we were flagged down by some uniformed men. They began searching the car thoroughly. I didn't feel we were in the slightest danger, so when they began going through the glove compartment, I asked the cab driver what they were looking for. He told me they were looking for a man. I said, "In the glove compartment?!" and was rapidly shushed by the car's occupants. We never learned just who the man was they were looking for, but I put my companions in some jeopardy with my big mouth.

I had great fun wandering around Havana in the daytime. One day I noticed that a funny little man was following me. After the first time I saw him, I never went anyplace without seeing this little man right behind me. I can't imagine that he was sent to spy on me because of my remark in the car, or if he was, he was a lousy gumshoe because I could always see him trotting along a few paces back.

Unbelievably I had another of those peeping toms in the hotel. As before, the bathroom was across from the transom. I was testing the bidet, and although I knew what it was for, I'd never seen one before. I turned on the faucet, leaned forward, and took a direct hit of water in my face. You didn't see a lot of bidets in Hamburg, Iowa. With water streaming down my face, I looked up at the transom, and once again, there was a face staring back at me. I threw on my robe, rushed into the hall, and saw no one except a little man sleeping in one of the chairs placed in the small upstairs sitting room. He had a hat over his face. Later I realized that the little man who had been following me was the same man I saw sleeping in the sitting room. He had obviously thrown himself into the chair and pretended to be sleeping when I rushed from the room.

Ralph Burns had a scary experience in Havana. He was sitting in the bar of the hotel one night when some lady of the evening began to talk to him. They had a few drinks, but Ralph made it clear he was not in the least interested. She was wearing the rattiest fur coat imaginable, and after Ralph left the bar, she reported to the police that he had stolen the coat. In Cuba you are guilty until proven innocent, so he was thrown into jail and spent a horrible night trying to reach Woody to bail him out. The moment he was free it all became funny, but at the time he was terrified.

Back in the States, I went on the road with Woody's small band for a few weeks. It was the same band, sans Dave Barbour. I wanted to sing "Everything Happens to Me," the Matt Dennis tune, but it was one of Bill Harris's favorite tunes to play. Neither of us would give it up so we took turns. Bill broke me up every night when, after the job, as he was walking back toward the band room, he played the first five notes of "Getting Sentimental Over You," the Tommy Dorsey theme song, purposely fluffing the final high note.

When Woody disbanded the small band, I went back to Los Angeles.

• 9 •

André Previn, Part One

I went back to Facks in San Francisco in the fall of 1950, this time singing with Cal Tjader's group. I had been in the club a few weeks and had built up quite a loyal following. Even better, the local musicians would come in to hear me after their gigs around San Francisco. That's the ultimate high—when your peers are interested enough to come to hear you. In fact, Paul Desmond came by almost every night, and who could ask for any better validation than that.

A disk jockey named Dale Wights, who worked for a local station and also volunteered his time on the Army's radio station at the Presidio, would come in to Facks almost every night. He told me that André Previn was in the Army and was stationed at the Presidio. Dale said he'd bring André into the club some Thursday night.

I knew very little about André, having the mistaken impression that he was English. I wasn't too fond of his piano playing—it was a bit too busy for me. Thursday came and Dale came in alone, telling me that André had gone to a big party in Hollywood that night but he'd bring him in the next week. This went on for several weeks until I ceased to care whether he brought him in or not. A few nights later Dale brought him in.

The night André finally turned up, he stayed for the entire evening. Some of the veterans of the Korean War were arriving on a troop ship at dawn the following morning, and I was scheduled to sing to them from aboard a ferry that would be maneuvered alongside the troop ship. After work that night, André and I went for some breakfast and drove out to the Golden Gate Bridge to watch the sun come up. Since it was nearing morning, we decided that André should come along on the ferry trip and accompany me on the piano.

As nearly as I can remember, it was "love at first sight" for us, so I was lucky to keep working in San Francisco, literally closing Facks one night and opening the next at the Blackhawk.

Our first date was dinner and the theater. Apparently André had borrowed money from his sergeant in order to finance the evening. He spent everything that night, and the sergeant couldn't believe it when André asked to borrow even more money!

André came into the club almost every night, and it had become my practice to play brushes on Cal's drums when he was playing vibes. André took one look at me and forbade me to play drums anymore. Hey, I coulda been Betty Rich!

One day André and I took a long drive up to Muir Woods. We drove all around the lovely area and managed to get lost. It was getting near to the time I was to be at work so I was really nervous. I cannot bear to be late. As we made a turn in a rural driveway, a peacock displayed his gorgeous tail feathers. It was a lovely and unforgettable moment. In the end I was quite late for work. The next day a dozen long-stemmed roses arrived at the hotel where I stayed. At that time billboards were all displaying ads for the railroad, with the caption, "Next time take the train." That was André's accompanying card with the flowers. Never having been given roses before, how was I to know that you don't chop off the long stems because they don't fit in a vase!

André was playing for me at the Blackhawk with Cal's group one night. In jazz, or popular music for that matter, there are four beats to a measure—unless you're talking about a waltz and I'm not—so it is very important to know where the first beat of the measure or "one" is. When I sing a ballad, I like it very slow so I can stretch out. The musicians have to concentrate, or they can lose their place. One night I started one of my ballads and Cal lost his concentration. I heard him mutter to André, "Hey man, where's 'one'?" That became a standing joke between Cal and me, and I don't think I ever saw him that he didn't repeat it.

On another occasion one of my ballads began with an arpeggio, after which I would start to sing. In the small pause between the arpeggio and my first note. I heard the bass player say to Cal, "Man, did that cat ever call you?" I was so fascinated with this that I forgot to come in altogether.

Vince Guaraldi was Cal's regular piano player in the Blackhawk, and he and Cal were good friends. A few years later Vince became famous and made a great deal of money writing the theme song and playing piano on the TV show and recording for *Peanuts*. I think Cal may have resented this to a certain extent because their friendship cooled. Someone asked me once if I knew why this had happened. "Yes," I said, "I think it was Peanuts envy."

Although I actually lived in Los Angeles, I spent so much time in San Francisco in the next year or so that, when André and I were finally married, I was described in the newspapers as "San Francisco singer, Betty Bennett."

The Army never knew what to do with André and set him to assembling boxes. This was such a demeaning occupation for him and such a waste of his talent. Nonetheless, they still kept him in the Army. My gig ended, and I went back to Los Angeles. We wrote to each other every day. Anyone who has ever had any kind of correspondence with André knows that he is a superb letter writer. I am sorry that once in a rage I destroyed all of his letters. It would have helped our daughters to understand that once we loved each other very much.

Eventually André was discharged and went back to MGM in his old capacity as composer/conductor. While he was doing his time in the Army, MGM was sending his parents a small sum of money each month. Upon his return to the studio he was informed that he was expected to pay back every penny. Patriotism was clearly not MGM's long suit.

It was early 1951 and I was beginning to get some attention from critics and record companies. My good friend Ralph J. Gleason was responsible for bringing me to the attention of *Downbeat* magazine, and as a result I won the "New Star of the Year" award. Things were beginning to look up for me, although it always amazed me to be paid for something that gave me so much pleasure. I would have been happy to do it for nothing.

With André back in Los Angeles, I had very little incentive to accept any work. MGM's insistence on being paid back for the money sent during André's Army hitch, and the fact that he lived at his parents' home and contributed to the household, made marriage impossible for the time being. I lived at home too, and my parents were wonderfully patient and remarkably generous about continuing to support a twenty-nine-year-old layabout.

I was under the impression when I met André—and he did nothing to disabuse me of this—that he was twenty-six. In fact, he was only twenty-two. Shortly before his twenty-third birthday, which I thought was his twenty-seventh, we were at his home. His mother and I were trying to sneak away from him to talk about what to do on his birthday. He kept following us around. I finally told him to leave us alone as we were planning his twenty-seventh birthday party. At this, his mother said, "You mean his twenty-third." I considered correcting her when it suddenly dawned on me: who would know his age better than his mother? I was devastated at this news and when we left the house André drove me all the way to the ocean, earnestly explaining that he was aware of how sensitive I was about my age and that he was afraid to tell me his correct age for fear I would stop seeing him. Of course he was right, but by now I was in love with him so it was too late to turn back. How the world has changed! Nobody gives a damn anymore. I, in fact, am all for May/December relationships, except a couple of times when I was December.

Just before André was discharged, MGM lowered everyone's salary. André felt that since he was still paying the studio back and was now earning even less money than before, it was impossible for us to marry. It was frustrating for us both, living with our parents, so André finally decided that if two couldn't live as cheaply as one, being poor together might make up for it. We set a date for August 1952.

Here I am with Mom and Dad, one year old.

Age five, posing

Fifteen, posing with my bass drum in my Hamburg Marching Band uniform

Mrs. Gladys Gottsche (with her son), my piano and vocal coach

Seventeen, graduation picture

Royce Stoenner and His Orchestra

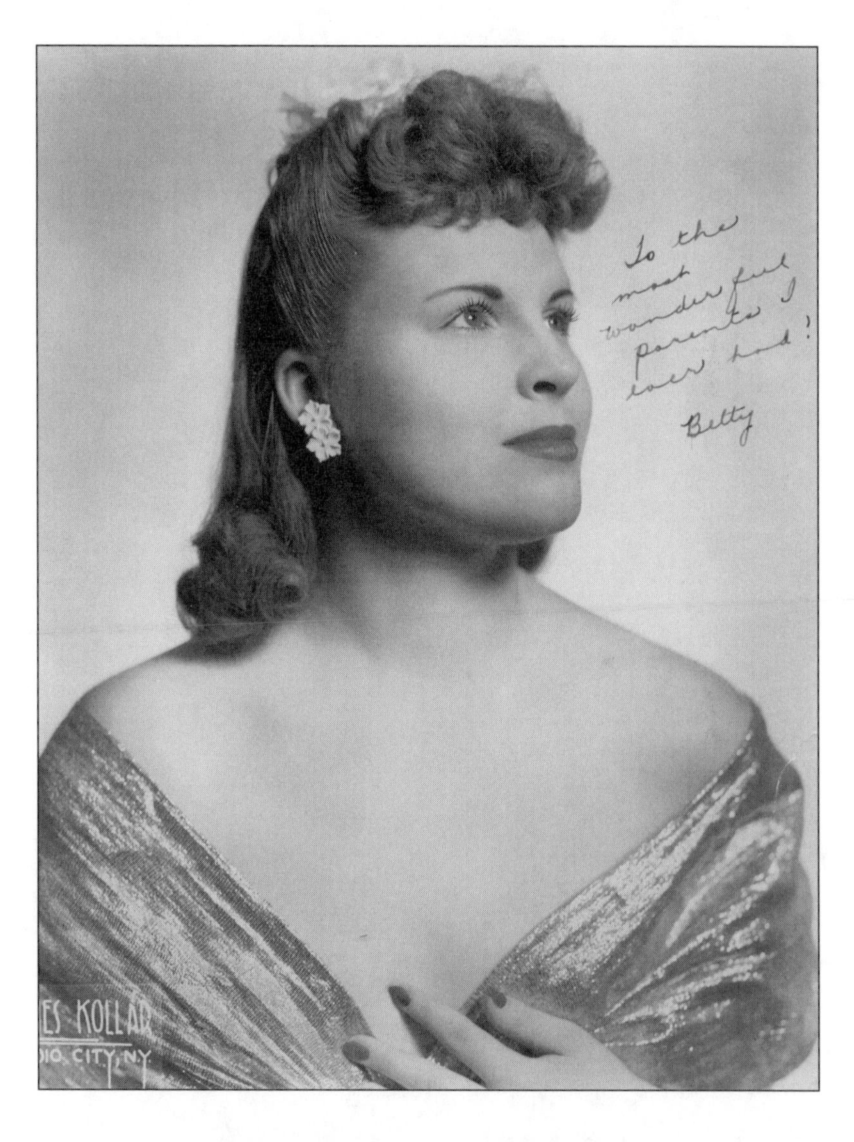

First professional picture, New York, 1941
Courtesy of James Kollar Studios, New York, N.Y.

Milt Page Quartet in Washington, D.C.

Milt Page Quartet in Atlantic City in 1943. Milt is at top right.
Courtesy of Atlantic Studios, Atlantic City, N.J.

Here I am in my Navy summer uniform, Hunter College, 1945.

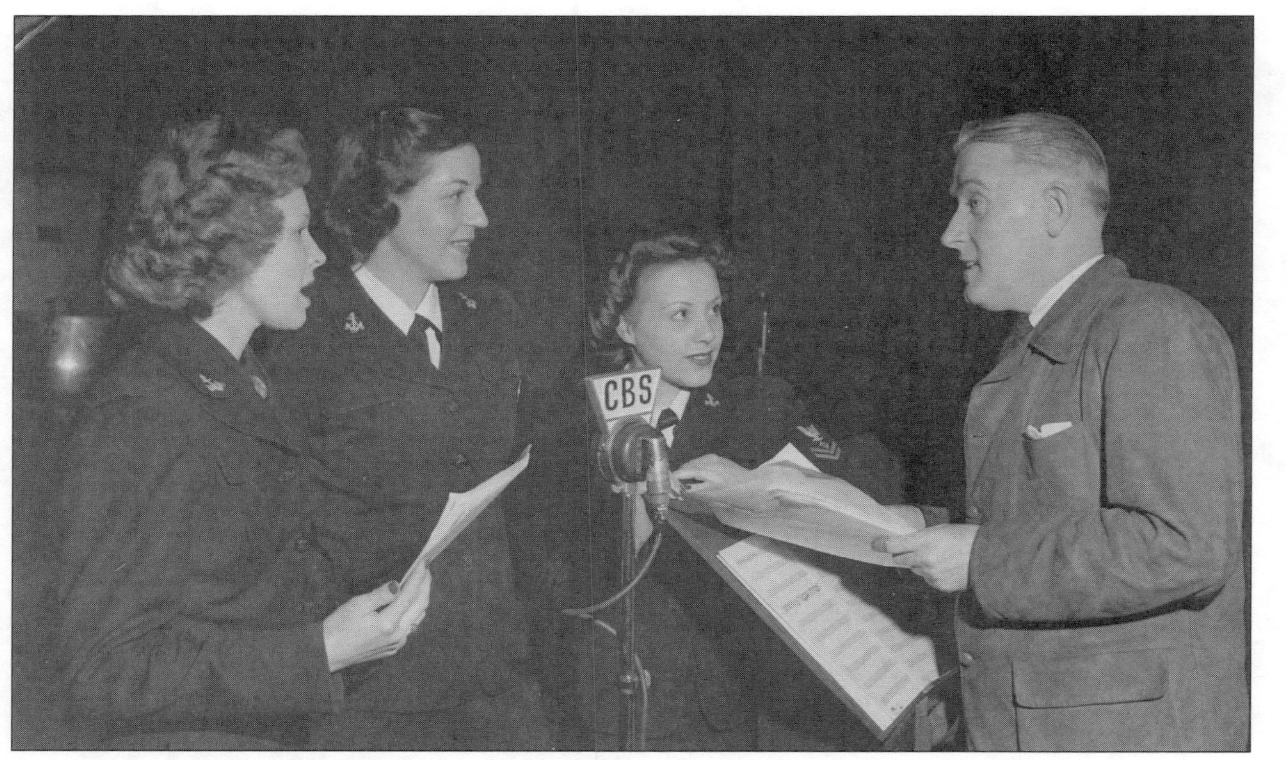

From right: Director Earle McGill, Donna Mason, Rosemary Schlack, and me, 1946

"Your Navy Date." I am posing to the right of the "bride." *Official U.S. Navy Photograph*

A poster for one of the hospital shows.

The Infamous Samba Quartet, 1945. *Official U.S. Navy Photograph*

Left to right: Pat Scudder, Rosemary Schlack, Ray Charles, me, and Donna Mason

Lt. Lou Mindling, William Shirer, and me, 1945
Official U.S. Navy Photograph

Standing in front of Boston Post Lodge (Claude Thornhill Band)

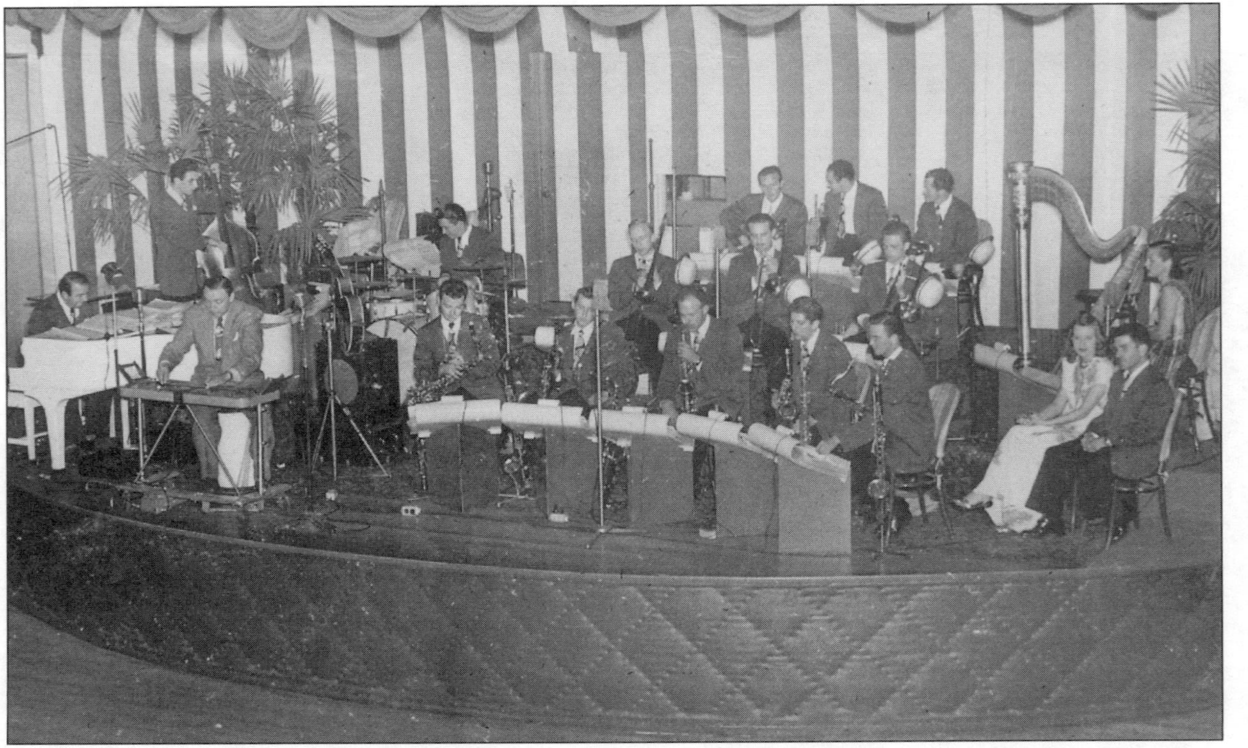

Alvino's band (1947), Jimmy Joyce (boy singer), and me. Rocky Cole on piano. Iggy Shevak, my first husband, on bass.

Alvino publicity photo, 1948
Courtesy of De Mirijan, New York, Hollywood

Vernon Alley Band. Richard Wyands, piano; Pony Poindexter, alto; Billy Stuart, drums; Alley, bass; and me. Facks, San Francisco, 1948
Courtesy of Down Beat

Charlie Ventura and me, 1949

Woody's group in Havana. *Left to right, front row*: Dave Barbour, Conte Candoli, Milt Jackson, Shelly Manne. *Back row*: two dancers, me, one dancer, Flip Manne, Woody, Abe Turchern (manager).

André Previn and I were married in August 1952 at John Green's house.

André and me in Carmel, 1953

André and me in concert, 1953
Courtesy of Steve Crouch, Carmel, Calif.

Claudia, André, Alicia, Beverly Hills, ca. 1960

Claudia, me, Alicia, Beverly Hills, ca. 1960

Publicity photograph, late 1950s

Publicity photograph, late 1950s

My parents, Radford and Doris Bennett, in London, 1964

Brian Auger, Babs Gonzales, Les Tomkins and me in London
in front of Ronnie Scott's Jazz Club

Mundell and I are reacting to Clark Terry's solo on our wedding night, 1975. Jimmy Lyons is to our left. *Courtesy of Roberto Morrison*

Mundell Lowe

Betty Bennett

• *10* •

Charlie Barnet

I began to feel guilty sitting idly around waiting for night to fall so I could see André again, and although my parents didn't say anything, I knew they must have been wondering how long it would be before I got moving. Luckily I heard from a friend that Charlie Barnet was going on the road for six weeks, and since this would take André and me up to the August wedding date, it seemed a good idea to try for the job. I met Charlie in his manager's office. He didn't ask me to audition; he just told me when and where to meet the departing bus.

One of our early gigs was in Corpus Christi, Texas. We played in a ballroom by the Gulf of Mexico for a week or two. My dressing room was on one side of the stage, the band's on the other. I sat alone in my dressing room between sets, listening to the sounds of hilarity emanating from the other dressing room. One night Charlie asked me to join the band in their dressing room. They were all drinking straight out of a bottle. Charlie looked up with a challenging expression on his face and said he was certain I wouldn't want a drink, that I probably didn't even drink. He told me that when Maryanne McCall sang with the band she always drank out of the bottle. I am not an especially bold person ordinarily, but if you dare me, I'm fearless. I snatched the bottle out of his hand and drank a few deep draughts. Instant acceptance. (And instant intoxication!) I'm sure he knew this was bravado on my part, but it did demonstrate that I was trying to be one of the cats on the band.

Although my time with the band was brief, I have the fondest memories of Charlie. He was kind, polite, gentlemanly, and never displayed any of the quirks for which he was famous.

Charlie had the nerve-wracking habit of standing in front and to the right of the microphone with his back to the audience, watching me every time I sang a tune. I just tried to do the best job I could, wondering if this was some sort of put-down or attempt to get me to break down. One night he asked me if I ever wondered why he stared at me while I was singing. I said yes. He told me that he was curious to see why so many people stood in front of the band while I sang, rather than dancing, so he was watching me to see if he could figure it out. He said that he didn't blame them—he could see why they liked to watch me. I was over the moon!

Charlie once asked me if I had heard about his bad reputation. I admitted that I had. He said that he had never given any problems to the singers on the band whom he respected and, as he respected me, I'd never have a problem. That kind of openness is so appealing and in those days it was quite unusual, especially from the bandleader! I think he enjoyed having the reputation he had for doing crazy things—or at least he didn't care what anyone thought. I assured him that I would keep the secret of how kind and thoughtful he'd been to me. I wouldn't dream of destroying his image.

We left Texas and did a series of incredible one-nighters. For some reason, possibly financial, we traveled on an ancient bus with no air-conditioning and a governor on the engine enabling the bus to travel no more than forty miles an hour. It was about a hundred in the shade, and we had five hundred miles to go to the next gig. The heat, flies, and overall discomfort generally bring out some of the best humor in the band members. The soldiers in World War II were famous for their black comedy, but they couldn't top some of the great cracks delivered during the grim times on the bus. As we crept along, I remember someone singing quietly "Onward Twisted Shoulders."

One of the memorable rest stops was in a ratty gas station outside a small town down south. The "restroom" consisted of a two-holer in back. The stench of the place was bad enough, but the worst part was that it was infested with bees—angry bees. There was no question of our finding another station because the bus was just about out of gas. We all used the "facilities" anyway, taking our lives (among other things) in our hands. With the aid of a little rapid dancing, nobody was stung. That brings up something that has puzzled me every time I play the south. There are signs in the ladies' restroom that say, "Please do not stand on seat." Why would anyone stand on the seat?

It's almost impossible to arrive at the job on time in a bus that travels at the breathtaking speed of forty miles an hour, so we knew we would never make it on time. In fact, we were a half hour late. The auditorium was full of restless customers. The band rushed up onto the bandstand still dressed in their travel clothes and began to play.

My road costume was too far gone, on the best of days, to be seen in, so I was hustled to the teachers' lounge to freshen up—a considerable operation after the long, hot trip. Some of the wives came with me, and one of them discovered that someone had upchucked in the washbasin. She kindly cleaned it out so I could wash up, apply makeup, and get into my gown. The teachers' lounge was at the back of the auditorium, so it was a long trip down the aisle and up the stairs to the backstage door and from there to the microphone. As I was combing my hair into a ponytail, I heard the band play a very familiar introduction—the introduction to a tune I sang! Clutching my ponytail in my right hand, having had no time to put a rubber band around it, I wildly rushed into the auditorium and up on the stage in time for my opening note. I didn't dare look at Charlie, but I could hear him snickering as I sang my chorus, still clutching my ponytail.

Our drummer left the band during the tour, but before he left, he gave me some very sensible advice about the element of surprise. I asked him if he had notified his wife when he would be returning or was he planning to pop in and surprise her. He said he thought that surprising her wasn't a good idea and would be very unfair. It robbed her of the chance to welcome him properly, and although he had no reason to distrust her, he didn't want to take a chance on coming in on something that might look worse than it actually was. So, gang, before you return home, keep those cards and letters coming. The surprise could be yours.

There were always a few musicians on every band I ever sang on who tried to shock me with their Rabelaisian humor. I sat in the front of the bus partly in order to give them as much freedom of speech as possible. If they persisted in using vile language, obviously directed toward me, I pretended not to understand, or I just ignored them. Happily, there were very few of these practitioners.

When I took the job with Charlie, we both understood that it would be for a couple of months—just until my wedding. The last night I was on the band we were driving from Fort Worth to Dallas, and Charlie asked me to ride in his Cord, along with the road manager. What a night! During the trip he asked me to stay with the band. He said the band was on its way to New York, and if I came with the band, he would do everything in his power to see that I got the recognition he thought I deserved. He suggested that I postpone my wedding, reminding me that with his marital record, I could see that he wasn't anti-marriage, but there was plenty of time for that. Now was a wonderful opportunity for me to do something with my singing career.

The Cord had bucket seats in front which were divided by a console. I sat in the passenger seat and the manager somehow managed to cram himself into the tiny back seat where he immediately fell asleep. The car was capable of traveling at (for then) a high rate of speed. During the trip, while Charlie was asking me to stay with the band, I was holding his bottle of booze, which, on request, I handed to him and he'd take a healthy slug. I tried to explain that I was in love and really wanted to get married and, since my wedding date had been set, I couldn't get out of it, nor did I want to. Charlie was adamant, however. This conversation took place as we sped down the highway at about one hundred miles an hour. Seventy-five would have been sufficient to frighten me—I'm terrified of speed. Suddenly Charlie opened the compartment between the seats and took out a gun. He spent the rest of the trip asking me if I was going to stay with the band, and when I said no, he would point the gun out the driver's window and shoot at the sky. From time to time the manager would open one eye in the back seat and say, "Cool it, Charlie," then go back to sleep. The scenario went like this: "Are you going to stay with the band?" "No," I would say firmly. Sound of gunfire. "Hand me the bottle." "Cool it, Charlie," from the backseat.

When we reached our destination, Charlie calmly wished me luck with my marriage and said that if I ever wanted to sing with his band I had only to give him a call and I could have the job back.

• 11 •

André Previn, Part Two

André and I spent a lot of time at Johnny and Bonnie Green's house. Johnny was the head of the music department at MGM where André was still under contract after he was discharged from the Army. Johnny was very fond of André, and when I told Bonnie that we planned to be married, she and Johnny insisted that we be married in their home. My father was working in Alaska at the time, so Johnny gave me away.

We were married in front of the fireplace, which was a free-standing affair serving as a partial room divider between John's special room containing his impressive recording equipment and the living room. To the left of the fireplace, the wall came up halfway, so it was possible to see into the part of the room that held the equipment. Saul Chaplin and my best friend, Carol Summerfelt, were our best man and maid of honor. During the ceremony, it was difficult not to be distracted by Johnny, who was standing to the left and in front of the technicians who were operating the recording equipment and playing the tapes as he alternately gave the bride away and directed the technician: hands up for louder, hands down for softer. We were later presented with a tape recording of the wedding, a cherished and thoughtful gift.

When André and I met, we were both involved with other people. One sad weekend I told my fellow about André; as agreed, André was to tell his lady at the same time. At the last minute he chickened out and didn't tell her. The day of the wedding we received dozens of telegrams, one of which was from this lady. She had apparently read about our wedding in the paper, and this was the first she had heard that she'd been replaced. At the time we all chuckled over it, but years later when I read about *my* replacement in the papers it didn't seem all that funny.

The only childhood disease I had escaped was the mumps. Shortly after the wedding, I somehow contracted it. The trouble was that André had never had mumps either, so two weeks after my recovery, he came down with them. Although his general health was fine, he had strep throat constantly. He had had his tonsils removed as a child in Germany, but for some reason they grew back. His German tonsillectomy had been a dreadful experience because his parents hadn't told him what was going to happen. When he realized why he was in the doctor's office, he was traumatized. He decided he'd rather suffer the sore throats than go through a second tonsillectomy. When the family doctor told him that he might present a danger to the child I was carrying, he agreed to have them taken out once more. Then, just before he was to play Gershwin's "Concerto in F" and "Rhapsody in Blue" with the Boston Pops Orchestra, he developed chicken pox! Once again I called our family physician. This would be the third childhood disease for which he had treated André. With just a touch of exasperation he said, "Have you thought of calling a pediatrician?"

André and I did have one insanity in common—even during a serious conversation. It was a sort of horrible compulsion to wrest an entirely different meaning from what was being said, instead of the one intended. It was a bit like hearing a few foreign phrases and trying to translate them into English. Word games were a part of our daily life, so much so that we spoke in a kind of shorthand made up of punch lines, Thurber captions, and outrageous puns.

When our oldest daughter married, André flew in from London for the wedding. The two of us and our two daughters were having lunch in a restaurant. Our daughters have inherited our compulsion. We all ordered salad. When the waiter appeared with it and said, "Would you like me to toss your salad?" we all looked at each other wildly and began to giggle. The waiter stood by helplessly, which only added to our hilarity. We knew we could never explain it so we didn't try.

My friends sometimes tease me unmercifully because I insist on being perfectly color-coordinated and always do a lot of fretting about being dressed properly for any occasion—even if it's only grocery shopping. There's no question that I am a fanatic on the subject. I'm sure it began during the Depression when I was five and we had very little money. My mother was a clever seamstress and made dresses for me out of old satin evening gowns she had worn while playing piano in clubs. Once I remember having a dress made from a coat lining. My little friends thought I was quite elegant, but I knew where my wardrobe came from and I was quite embarrassed. I was eleven years old before I had a store-bought coat.

This insecurity was exacerbated after my marriage to André when his friends became my friends and mine, his. His friends, however, were at the top in their professional lives and always exquisitely and expensively dressed. On the rare occasion when I was dressed more or less according to the dress code of the evening, I was, nonetheless, ill at ease. I definitely did not fit into the group of designer-gowned ladies, one of whom once said to me, "Have you been in that divine little scarf shop outside Paris?" Paris! I was a recent graduate of Lerners of Long Beach!

A group of Hollywood entertainers had gone to Korea to do a series of shows for the soldiers. They had become quite fond of the officer who was their official host on the tour, and when the officer came to town, Danny and Sylvia Kaye gave a party in his honor. Although André had not gone to Korea with them, we were asked to attend the gathering. I was told the dress was "casual," so I wore a very nice gray flannel dress with white collar and cuffs and matching gray flannel spectator pumps (very Kitty Foyle). When we arrived, I was horrified to see that all the women wore sequins or better. The Kayes' den contained a sofa that ran the length of the room. I sat all alone in the center of this sofa for most of the evening, while the glittering guests talked over old Korea times. André was in the living room playing the piano. At least it gave him something to do with his hands.

There was a very elegant club on La Cienega Boulevard in Los Angeles, called John Walsh's 551 club. Julie London began her singing career there, and I was excited to be booked into the club. The film composers and their wives and other celebrities came in to hear me. It took me a little time to settle down, but finally I felt secure. One night two men came in dressed in black suits, black shirts, and white ties. I realized that one of the men was Swifty Lazar, a famous agent whom I'd met through André. I decided to show him that I wasn't just André's little wife, but a good singer. I am seldom completely happy with my performance, but that night I felt good about the show. Presently I went to the table to say hello to Swifty, and to my astonishment and fright, his companion was Frank Sinatra! I was grateful that I hadn't known he was there before the show.

They invited me to sit down. Frank asked if I wanted a drink. I said I didn't drink. He offered me a cigarette, and I said I didn't smoke. He looked at me as if there was little hope. Shortly after, he and Swifty got up to leave, and Frank said they were going to a friend's saloon. (Some saloon! Mike Romanoff's very exclusive restaurant in Beverly Hills!) Frank invited me to come with them. I briefly considered asking André for a divorce just for the night so I could! As Frank was leaving, he shook my hand warmly, complimented me on my singing, and wished me the best of luck. To my eternal humiliation, I wished him the best of luck, too. He happened to be working on the MGM lot where André was under contract. I begged André to look him up the next day and assure him that I wasn't as dumb as I sounded! Imagine wishing Frank Sinatra the best of luck!

The next night just as I was being announced, in came Frank again with a girl singer he was dating at the time. I can only say I did the best I could, considering the trembling I was doing under my gown! Jimmy Rowles played piano for me, and Bob Bertout played bass. Shorty Rogers's wife, when told the name of the bass player, misunderstood and asked me if I was using a girl on bass. I asked her why she thought I was. She said, "Isn't her name Barbara Toe?" I never addressed Bob Bertout again as anything but Barbara.

The marriage effectively put my singing career on hold, although I was always being asked to sing at parties we attended. There was usually someone there who was determined to get me into the movies. Although I was "discovered" about once a month, nothing ever came of it. The closest I came was when a singer was needed to sing "Suppertime" during the main title of a movie. It looked promising until the producer decided to use a black singer. How could I complain? It was Carmen McRae!

After dinner one evening at the Greens, also attended by Ira and Lee Gershwin, I was asked to sing. Panicky but game, I sang "Someone to Watch Over Me," one of George and Ira's tunes. I cherish the comment he made to André about me when I had finished. He said, "I only wish George could have heard her." That same evening I sang "Over the Rainbow." I had been singing this song for years, and it had evolved into a very different melody from the one Harold Arlen had written. I had no sooner sung the last note when Johnny spoke up. "What's the matter, isn't Harold Arlen's melody good enough for you?" I was absolutely crushed until Ira said ever so mildly, "Well, Johnny, I think we all pretty much know the melody to 'Over the Rainbow' by now and I think it is wonderful to hear what a jazz singer can do with it."

Judy Garland told us this story. She ran into Ira in Beverly Hills the day after he heard me sing "Over the Rainbow." He told her that he heard someone sing "Over the Rainbow" the night before better than anyone extant. Patently untrue, of course, but how graceful of Judy Garland to tell this on herself. That song belonged to her, and she and everyone else knew it.

One of the musicians under contract at MGM had died while on vacation, and the entire orchestra turned out for the funeral. Attending a funeral today is very different from the way it was twenty-five years ago. People are no longer all dressed in black. We all dress much the same as we would for an evening out. Funerals are so unnatural that it is difficult to assume the proper demeanor. This is especially so with musicians. Probably because it is so at odds with the somewhat cynical, jocular way they are with each other. In the old days when the black suit was de rigueur at funerals, it was not a wardrobe problem for a musician, because after he got his union card his next purchase was a black suit for club dates. Of course, by working in the suit nightly it had become a bit shiny and was redolent of stale smoke and the general nightclub stench. The occupant of the suit looked pale, tired, uneasy, and seemed to be very far away.

Although André and I barely knew the fallen musician, we attended the funeral out of respect for his widow and the rest of the orchestra. During the interludes (if you will) a string quartet made up of members of the MGM orchestra played some lovely chamber music from behind a curtain up front. Then they played "Our Love Is Here to Stay," which had been specially arranged for them by one of the arrangers in the MGM orchestra. It had been the musician and his wife's favorite tune. The quartet played it so beautifully that both André and I cried.

Later, in the parking lot, André complimented the concert master of the string quartet. We have prized his classic response lo these many years. He said, "Thank you, André, but it was a bad room." André beat a hasty retreat to our car to keep from laughing out loud.

In the early fifties, Georgie Auld made a series of albums with strings. They were quite wonderful and got a lot of air play. André wrote some of the arrangements and conducted the orchestra. I was present at the first record date. In those days, string players dressed and behaved differently from jazz musicians. They weren't telling ribald jokes and discussing chicks. Instead, they ran scales as well as other warmup methods. Georgie appeared at the door wearing a beautifully tailored pinstriped suit with the exaggerated shoulders worn in those days. He had on highly polished moccasins, a shirt with the Billy Eckstine collar—three inches wide—and a very nice tie done in a Windsor knot. He was carrying his saxophone in a canvas sack and looked unbelievably hip. He looked around at the string players in semi-amazement and said to André, "Which one of those cats is Ray Nance?" (For those of you who don't know who Ray Nance is, he played fiddle and trumpet with Duke Ellington.)

Later on I amended my impression of classical players. During a playback at a recording in the Goldwyn studio, André and I were standing with Red Mitchell and a couple of the string players, one of whom looked dreadful. When André commented on this, he said that he had been in bed with the flu the night before when his friend called and said he was with two chicks and wanted him to join them. The flu-ridden player told him he was simply too ill to do it. His friend insisted, explaining that his chick wouldn't go without her friend, so the musician struggled out of his sickbed and joined them. André said he couldn't understand why, if he was so ill, he would consent to do this. After a thoughtful pause, Red Mitchell said solemnly, "It's the law of the road."

Although I had had favorable critical acclaim, I never seemed to be in the right band at a time when they were recording the girl singer. When I was with Thornhill, they were pushing the boy singer. With some of the other bands, there were no current record contracts. I did do some recording with Alvino Rey's band, but I was almost an afterthought in the arrangement. I recorded a few forgettable sides with Charlie Ventura. With André I was able to record my first album for Trend Records. André wrote some beautiful string arrangements and played celeste on the dates. We used a string quartet with oboe and flute and rhythm section. The string quartet was an interesting and impressive mix—each player was a concert master. We did some beautiful but (back then) obscure ballads. The album received rave reviews, but was not commercial enough for that time.

André and I used to browse in a small neighborhood record shop in Beverly Hills. The clerk was familiar with us from our frequent visits. One day André was in there alone, and Duke Jordan, a well-known pianist and arranger, came in. The clerk came up to André, holding my album, and jokingly said, "Mr. Previn, here's an album you might like." Whereupon Duke said, "Oh man, Brownie [Clifford Brown] carries that album on the road with him. I don't see what he sees in her." André said, "You mean my wife?" Duke said hastily, "Well, actually the chick's okay, it's those arrangements." André said, "You mean my arrangements?" The next scene was Duke Jordan, a beaten man, slinking out of the record shop. When André related this story to me, I laughed heartily—a little too heartily. I thought it was funny, but at the same time it infuriated me. My reaction can best be understood if you've ever heard the famous Woody Herman line: "There are three sexes: men, women, and girl singers."

The next album with André was for Atlantic Records, with the arranging chores split between Shorty Rogers and André. And what a band! Shorty on trumpet; Frank Rosolino on trombone; Harry Klee on alto and flute; Bob Cooper on tenor sax; Jimmy Giuffre on baritone sax; Barney Kessel, Ralph Pena, and Shelly Manne in the rhythm section. On the ballads we added Arthur Gleghorn, flute; Phil Memoli, oboe; Gus Bivona, clarinet; Dave Pell, bass clarinet; John Cave, French horn; and Catherine Johnk, harp. Once again, great reviews but little else.

The last album I recorded with André was after we were divorced. It was for United Artists and we used a rhythm section. Although I have always gotten good reviews on my albums, I have never made one I liked until a CD I made with Mundell recently.

Meanwhile, back at the marriage. Since childhood I have been an avid reader but with no direction whatsoever. I read whatever I could pick up on the road. Although I had a library card, I was seldom in town long enough to use it. André suggested reading material for me. (Shades of F. Scott and Sheila!) At one point I settled down to read *War and Peace*, loving every chapter of it. André remarked that he'd never before known anyone who "couldn't put down" *War and Peace*.

My familiarity with classical music was confined to the course in Music Appreciation (a misnomer if there ever was one) I took when I was twelve years old in elementary school. I thought it was boring. André opened this door for me, acquainting me with his favorite composers, so that eventually I was able to recognize composers even though I may not have heard that particular work before.

I have always been (scrupulously) honest. I wouldn't dream of taking a hotel towel or ashtray—with one glaring exception. André and some of the MGM stars were appearing, mostly under protest, at an American Legion dinner. We were all picked up in a magnificent stretch limousine, everyone dressed to the nines and up. (I was, as usual, dressed to about the sevens.) There were endless speeches by representatives of the legion, and the MGM people waited for hours in the employees' dining room. The tables were set up for the next meal with silverware and napkins at each place. Perhaps out of boredom or resentment at the long wait, I committed my first (and only) illegal act. We had just moved into our new home and had only a few mismatched pieces of silver. I quietly slipped four place settings under my mink stole. In the limousine on the way home I displayed my ill-gotten gains to André. He was thunderstruck and horrified.

A few months later, after we had acquired a full complement of silver, I boxed up the stolen goods and sent them back to the hotel. I did not include a return address. I like to contemplate the bewilderment of the employee who opened the package.

Of all the people I met through André, the film composers and their wives were my favorites. Hugo Friedhofer, Herb Spencer, Earle Hagen, Conrad Salinger, Lennie Hayton, Cyril Mockridge, and Miklos Rosza. I was a nervous and inexperienced hostess so I began my entertaining by giving a champagne brunch. We all had a hilarious time, thanks to the champagne. In fact, these champagne brunches became very popular.

The composers' wives decided to meet each Monday for lunch, one month of Mondays in each restaurant. It was a loose arrangement, whereby you appeared if you were available, no "regrets" necessary. One day I came home from a shopping excursion to find a note from my cleaning lady. It read (I swear): "The ladies are meeting at the Cock and Balls next Monday."

In 1953 I became pregnant with our first daughter, Claudia. So that the trip to the hospital would go off without a hitch (and because we were both a little hysterical), we made a few dry runs. At that time Jack Wagner (Roger Wagner's brother) was a disk jockey for a local station, and he often played tunes from both André's piano albums and my vocal album. André had an early appointment one morning in Beverly Hills. I awakened before he did, felt the first twinge, and knew that labor was beginning. The thought of putting André through the long hours of waiting seemed unnecessary, so I sent him off on his appointment without telling him about my cramps. I called my mother to come and wait with me. That day Jack alternately played one of my tunes, then one of André's for his entire program, announcing that the birth of our first child was imminent. He had no idea how imminent! When the doctor said it was time for me to go to the hospital, I called André and he raced home. Mario Andretti would have been hard put to keep up with us on the way to the hospital. Claudia, however, wasn't born until 9:30 that night. It just struck me that she has been late ever since.

In 1951, when André first returned to MGM after his hitch in the Army, he met one of the contract players, a very good singer/actress MGM was grooming. This lady had a major crush on André. By the time he was aware of it, he and I were engaged, so it went nowhere. In 1956 I was pregnant with our second daughter, Alicia. During the sixth week of my pregnancy, André went to San Francisco to play at the Blackhawk. Who should be appearing at the Fairmont but the singer/actress? They fell into each other's arms. A wife in the morning sickness phase of pregnancy is very little competition for an eager, young, smitten woman. By the time I came up for the last couple of days of André's engagement, the marriage was over. I just didn't know it yet.

Back in Los Angeles, André would come home from MGM and sit alone in the living room, reading. He barely spoke to Claudia and me. We'd huddle in the den and wonder what became of Papa. It never occurred to me to ask him why he was behaving the way he did. I suppose the reason was that I have always protected myself by never asking a question to which I'm afraid of the answer. A common complaint today is the lack of communication between couples. After five years of role-playing husband and wife, André and I never really knew each other.

The Bennetts have a family tradition of patting each other, sometimes for comfort, sometimes to show affection and pride. I brought this tradition to my marriage and later to our children. Long after the marriage ended, André confessed to me that he hated being patted—it made him feel like a child. Why didn't he tell me? Occasionally he would tell me something I knew was untrue. I never questioned it. Later, during my pregnancy and after our separation, when I was seeing the psychologist, I grumbled to him about this. He told me I was as much to blame as André because I never challenged him, thus perpetuating the problem.

Claudia and I endured a few weeks of the silent treatment, and finally one evening at dinner I asked André what was troubling him.

He said that he was dissatisfied with the way his career was going and didn't know what direction he should take. I suggested that he move into a hotel for a couple of weeks until he could sort things out. Later, as the papers began printing stories about André and his new lady, the reason for the silent treatment became very clear.

In the months to come, my outraged friends often talked about André's bad timing in leaving me during my pregnancy, but I would have found it too demeaning to ask him to stay until after the baby was born. I had my father and mother, who comforted and nurtured me through this agonizing period, and when labor began, my mother drove me to the hospital. As I filled out the admission papers between labor pains, she began to cry. The admitting nurses were brusque and cold. They have a lot to learn about the bedside (or desk side) manner. I suppose I derived a certain bizarre pleasure out of being a Poor Soul.

The moment I realized there was another woman I wanted to file for divorce immediately. André's father begged me not to. The family was convinced this would be a short-lived relationship and asked me to hold off on a divorce to protect André from rushing into another marriage. André's sister suggested to him that he go into therapy, and as is the custom, the psychologist wanted to speak to me. He felt strongly that it was important for me to go into therapy with André, partly because he felt that the birth of the baby would be traumatic for me and partly as an effort to get us back together, or at least to help me through the pregnancy. André has always had a problem facing up to unpleasant encounters—a trait he shares with a lot of men—so the psychologist felt it was important to make André face up to asking me for a divorce. An exercise in character-building, I guess.

In fact, the romance didn't last, nor did André ask me for a divorce. He was leaving for Paris to score the movie *Gigi* and I suggested that this would be a good time for me to see an attorney about a divorce. He asked me to wait until he returned from Paris, and maybe we could work out our problems. Eleven weeks later, when he did return, we realized that too much had happened between us, and neither of us were all that interested in salvaging the marriage.

After our divorce, I was constantly asked if it had been difficult to live with André. Nothing could be farther from the truth. He was (and is) great to be around. He is loving, generous, very bright, and terribly funny.

André didn't have a standard childhood in Germany. At age four his father discovered that André had perfect pitch, and the piano lessons began at once. With Nazism on the rise, it was too dangerous to play a simple game of "hide and seek" on the street, especially for Jewish children. "Hide and seek and kill" would have been a better name for it. Perhaps as a result of having had no childhood, André sometimes displayed a childlike wonder at the most commonplace things. One evening at a friend's house he accompanied the hostess to the kitchen where she planned to prepare cinnamon toast. She got out some bread, turned on the broiler, and shoved the bread under it. After a moment André said, "That's amazing. How do you know it's going to be cinnamon toast when it comes out?" Another time he ran through the virtues of having a refrigerator which keeps things cold. "How would it be," he said, "to have an appliance which could keep things hot?" I said, "You mean, like the stove?"

The divorce had a devastating effect on our younger daughter, Alicia. Out of an overwhelming desire for a father, at age sixteen she joined a small religious cult. The guru was a hypnotic man and the strong father figure she so desperately missed. She was a natural recruit. As a baby she had been fiercely independent, even refusing to be held and fed her bottle when only five months old. I was reduced to buying her a bib which held the bottle, and as she drank it, I paced the hall, wringing my hands, wondering how Dr. Spock would have handled it.

As Alicia grew older and began staying overnight with her girlfriends, the friend's father would tell me that she had asked him to be her father. When he reminded her that she already had a father, she told him she wanted a father who "lived on the premises." Claudia, on the other hand, was not an independent child, but nonetheless fared much better despite the absence of a resident father. How strange that the independent child would develop such a powerful need for a father, while the dependent child has always seemed reasonably content to see her father only occasionally. Now that they are older, they tell me that I was wrong about both of them. They long for their father, who has always lived either in England or on the East Coast, while they both live in California. Add to this a crippling conducting schedule, and it's nearly impossible for them to stay close to him. He tries to make up for it with telephone calls.

I have long since recovered from any bitterness I felt toward André. I always secretly felt that if he'd been there for Alicia she might not have joined the cult. It took a very long time for André and Alicia to work out their differences once she came home. She has since married, and we now have a lovely grandson. André is married to an attractive British woman, and they also have a young son. At the time André was married, he was still living in England. He called us to announce his marriage and ruefully reminded me that it was his fourth. I told him not to worry about it. I've been married four times, so he should do what I did: keep doing it until you get it right!

• *12* •

Benny Goodman

After the divorce in 1958 from André I bought a small house in what I called the slums of Beverly Hills. During our marriage I often heard members of the exclusive Beverly Hills community speaking disparagingly about those déclassé folks who lived south of Sunset. According to them, the "correct" place to live was north of Sunset, so it was with considerable pride I pointed out that my new address was, indeed, north of Sunset. However, when I recited my address to one of these experts I learned that my house was about a half-mile too far north of Sunset—hence, "slums."

I came home from a shopping trip one day and found a note asking me to call long distance operator number twenty. I was given a phone number. André happened to call me, and when I mentioned the number to him, he said, "That's Benny Goodman's number in Connecticut." It reminded me of the old joke about the musician who called home and was told by his roommate that he had a telegram from Benny Goodman. In a high state of excitement he asked his roommate to open the wire and read it. The wire read: "Stay where you are, signed, Benny." Of course I thought André was putting me on when he said the number was Benny's, but when I called it, there was no mistaking Benny's voice.

He said the band was going on a six- to eight-week tour and his former singer, Martha Tilton, had been scheduled to do it but for some reason had decided not to. The band had already been rehearsing in New York for a few days, and Benny had asked his pianist, Russ Freeman, the West Coast pianist (and a friend of mine) if he knew of a singer who could replace Martha on short notice. Russ went out, bought the album I made with Shorty and André, and played it for Benny. He decided to use me on the tour and asked me to bring a couple of the arrangements from the album with me.

I was ecstatic about getting the call from Benny, even though I was very aware of Benny's reputation for destroying girl singers. He was a marvelous clarinet player, respected and admired by all musicians for his abilities as a player, but his callous treatment of his sidemen was well known. I asked him for what I thought was an exorbitant amount of money, sure that he'd turn me down. He didn't.

I flew to New York City the day before the band left on tour, so there was no time for me to rehearse with the band. My rehearsal was set up for the afternoon of the first evening concert.

The band flew to New England where we picked up a bus in which we traveled from job to job in the New England territory. At the end of the New England jobs, we flew to the Midwest, picked up a bus, and worked around that territory. This routine was repeated all around the country. This was not a standard ballroom dance band-type tour. We played concert dates almost exclusively, usually in the same halls in which the local symphonies performed.

Benny was traveling on the bus with the band, a relatively rare occurrence with leaders. He sat next to me. He called me the "chantoosie." At my first rehearsal with the band we ran down a couple of the arrangements I had brought. They were both fast tempo. He hadn't asked for the arrangements on any of the ballads on my album, so when he asked me what ballad I wanted to sing I suggested Matt Dennis's lovely song, "Angel Eyes." As I had no big band arrangement of the tune, I sang it with just Russ Freeman and the bass and drums. During the ten minutes it took to run the tune down, Benny lay flat on his back on the floor of the stage, hands folded over his chest, eyes closed. It was unnerving. After I finished, he lay there for a few more minutes, opened his eyes, and said, "Are you finished?"

The routine on one of the arrangements I brought was that I sing the first chorus, then the band changes keys and plays a chorus, then back to my key with a final vocal chorus and a tag. That night on the stage, after I had sung my first chorus, the band swung into the new key and got steadily worse. Benny was so upset by the cacophony that he waved me back to the microphone sixteen bars before the band got to my key change. In a concert hall, full of hundreds of adoring Goodman fans, I didn't have the nerve to tell Benny to wait for my key change, so I went back to the microphone and tried to fake the tune in the band's key. By this time the band and I were in such disarray that before the arrangement ended, Benny simply stopped the band. Not an auspicious beginning. Later we discovered that some brilliant lighting person backstage had decided the stage was too bright, so he dimmed the lights and the band couldn't see the parts. It was no wonder it sounded so dreadful.

Next came my ballad. I was so embarrassed about the mixup on my first tune, which the audience undoubtedly thought was my fault, that I gave it my all and the audience reaction seemed to vindicate me.

After the concert that night, Benny asked to see Russ Freeman and me in his dressing room. He asked me where I had found the song "Angel Eyes." I told him Matt Dennis had written it. Benny said that, as he had never heard of it, it couldn't be much of a tune. Russ tried to save me by telling him that Ella Fitzgerald had recorded it. It didn't help. Although I continued to sing "Angel Eyes" throughout the tour, and always with great audience response, we never again played any of the arrangements I brought along. That night Benny announced a special rehearsal for me to take place the afternoon of the following day in the next town.

Crushed, I walked out of Benny's dressing room and headed for the bus. The band was lined up alongside the bus, and as I passed them, they all patted me and told me to hang in there.

At rehearsal the next afternoon, Benny dug out a few of his old arrangements for me. One of them was the Cole Porter tune "Ridin' High," an arrangement that had been written for Benny and Ella Fitzgerald. This was not only an unfamiliar arrangement, it was a tune that I had never heard before.

The standard song is thirty-two bars long, split into eight-bar phrases. The first and second eight bars are identical; then comes the middle eight, or bridge, which is entirely different. The last eight bars are like the first and second eights. Porter changed the format in "Ridin' High." The first and second sections are sixteen bars long instead of eight, and the bridge is only fifteen bars, making it difficult to "feel." I had the problem of not only learning the melody of the song, but the lyrics as well, in order to perform it on a concert stage that night.

Russ Freeman spent the afternoon after the band left, patiently running the tune over and over with me. It paid off, because that night I got through it and the rest of the new (to me) arrangements, but at a considerable cost to my nervous system.

Aside from a long engagement at Mister Kelly's in Chicago and a couple of dates at the Hungry i in San Francisco, I hadn't been singing much. I'd been staying home raising my two daughters. I was unable to afford lavish evening gowns, so I went to Jax in Beverly Hills, where I bought most of my clothes, and had them make me four identical outfits in four different colors. They were silk, ruffled bullfighter's shirts, worn with high-waisted, closely fitted long velveteen skirts, much like the hobble skirts worn years ago. Velveteen matching suspenders buttoned onto the skirts with large pearl buttons. One side of the skirt was slit to the knee. They were so different from the traditional low-cut, sequined gowns worn by the singers Benny was accustomed to seeing that he insisted that I fly ahead to Boston—the site of our next job—to buy a couple of suitable gowns. Everything was so expensive that, in the end, I bought just one, which I had to wear every night. The band was wonderful about it. Every night when I'd appear, they'd comment on my lovely new gown. I finally called my mother in California and asked her to send me a couple of additional dresses. However, our schedule was such that it was a month before they arrived.

That wasn't the least of my worries. Benny continued to ride on the bus with us. One night the band cornered me and said Benny was only riding on the bus because he fancied me. They said, "Look, either sleep with him or tell him you're not going to. Otherwise, we'll never get him off the bus." Benny had never suggested anything of the kind to me, but after a week or so, he began traveling in a private car. He made me pay for it later.

I did have one interesting conversation with him before he departed the bus. He asked me if I found it a little frightening, coming back to singing after such a long time away. Of course I admitted I did. He confessed that he had the same problem—he was as apprehensive as I was. He certainly didn't show it.

Benny was one of the first bandleaders to use racially mixed bands. It took courage to do this in the old days. Today there are laws forbidding hotels to refuse rooms to blacks, but we were traveling in areas that flouted this law. Once again the bus drove to the "black" neighborhood, dropped off part of the band, and drove on to the "white" hotels.

One of the musicians was a well-respected music educator/trumpet player from San Francisco. He had never experienced the kind of prejudice in San Francisco he found in St. Louis. He and a few of the musicians went out for dinner in a highly recommended restaurant and were turned away with some flimsy excuse about reservations. His dinner companions were heartsick that they had inadvertently put him in this humiliating position.

One night the band had gone into the hall to start the concert, and I ran back to the bus having forgotten something. Turk Van Lake, the guitarist, was sitting in his seat, looking disconsolate. When I asked him what was wrong, he said that his zipper was stuck—he couldn't get it to go up or down. I told him that he had just lucked out as I am one of the premier zipper-fixers. He expressed some embarrassment at having to remove his trousers, but I assured him that wouldn't be necessary. The bus floor was on one level, the seats one step up. As I was kneeling on the step, intent on repairing the zipper, my head bent over Turk's fly, a couple of the musicians came back on the bus, saw what they thought was a sexual encounter, and began to back out hurriedly, making apologies as they fled. Turk and I decided not to enlighten them.

Each night on the way to the gig, the band would have the bus driver stop at a liquor store so they could stock up. The band would always ask if I was coming in with them. I explained to them that I wasn't much of a drinker, so I always declined. But after two uneasy weeks with the band, when the bus pulled up to a liquor store before the gig, I was the first one off the bus!

I would guess that a quiet camaraderie develops on all of the Goodman bands, because you all know that sooner or later you're going to get it from Benny. We marveled at Turk Van Lake, who escaped Benny's wrath for weeks. We couldn't understand it. He told us that his night would come, and, of course, it did.

When Zoot Sims was about eighteen, he was playing with Benny at the New Yorker Hotel. Zoot must have led a charmed life because Benny never gave him the slightest problem. Every night Benny would come in, pat Zoot's head, and say, "Hello, kid." One night Zoot brought an apple which he placed on his music stand. Shortly after, Benny picked up the apple and ate it.

Terry Gibbs says that he can do an unlimited number of talk shows, just telling his Benny Goodman stories. Any time three musicians get together, eventually the Benny Goodman stories begin to pour out. In fact, one of the funniest happened to Mundell. He has played with Benny many times, and on this occasion he was doing the Socony Gas Show with Benny's band. That afternoon the sound man set him up on a stool in the curve of the piano. One minute before air time Benny said, "Hey, kid, move back behind the piano next to the bass." Mundell told him there was no time before the show, but Benny absolutely insisted. Mundell carefully watched the clock, and when the hand swept up to one second before air time, he roughly unplugged his guitar. The sound man in the booth jumped about three feet. Mundell loudly packed up his guitar and amp and stomped out while Benny was trying to play the theme. Popsy Randolph (Benny's famous band boy) rushed after Mundell, telling him he couldn't walk out. I can't repeat what Mundell answered. The very next week Benny called Mundell for the show as if nothing had happened. Mundell played it, too.

At the end of one of the arrangements I sang with the band, Benny and I played and sang a little unison bebop phrase. I am not fond of the syllables that most scat singers use and think that musicians, just in demonstrating a lick, use much better ones, so at the end of the tune I sang some syllables that were more consistent with those a musician might use. At first, Benny would just look at me strangely when he heard what I was singing, but after a couple of nights he would play the phrase with me in what can best be described as "ricky-tick." Then he'd use that comic laugh that clarinet players can do on their horns.

After the job I'd get into my traveling clothes and head for the bus. The band would once again be lined up along the bus. Every night I'd ask them if what Benny had said or done to me that night was directed toward "the girl singer" in general or toward me, Betty Bennett. They would assure me that this was his standard treatment toward the girl singer, and I made a vow that he'd never make me cry unless the slur was directed toward me, personally.

We played at Iowa State University, and the school had a pleasant little vocal group which sang a few tunes with our band. Being local is always a great advantage to a performer. The group tore the house down. Benny hired them to fly in over each weekend to perform with the band. It was a wonderful break for them, but terrible for me. Before long, the girl who sang lead in the group was singing solos with the band, preceded by an incredible buildup by Benny. He would tell the audience that the girl was only eighteen and describe what a great singer she was. I longed to quit the band, but I would have had to pay my fare home, so I stuck it out.

After the girl sang her tunes, it was time for me. I was now singing a couple of the famous old Goodman hits like "Bei Mir Bis Du Schoen" and "And the Angels Sing." I enjoyed them as much as the public did during their era, but they were just a drag to me under the circumstances. Benny's introduction for me now consisted of "And now, the girl who sings with the band." No name.

Two days before the tour ended, we worked a one-day theater. After the last show I ran upstairs and removed my makeup and donned my traveling clothes. (We were driving on to the next and final concert and had not checked into a hotel that day.) Word came from Benny that after the band played its last tune he wanted us all to be introduced once again so that we could take an additional bow. I asked to be excused because it would mean putting on my gown again and, worse, reapplying all of my stage makeup. Benny refused to excuse me. So, grumbling, I redid myself and ran downstairs to stand in the wings with the rest of the acts. Benny introduced the members of the band, the additional acts, and the vocal group, but he neglected to mention me. I was left standing in the wings. It did seem to me that this time the slur was definitely directed at me, Betty Bennett, so I ran upstairs sobbing wildly, rushed into the dressing room, and locked the door. The road manager spent thirty minutes coaxing me out. Benny later tried to apologize for this, but it was far, far too late by then.

When I returned to California, my stress-related fever sores broke out again with a vengeance! They spread over my chin this time, and I was an untouchable for about six weeks. It became a game among my friends to get me to talk about my tour with Benny because, after refusing the first few times they asked, I'd start my stories, becoming more and more agitated as I went along. Finally, they would all break up, and I'd realize that I'd been had again.

André told me that some months later Benny called him and asked for my telephone number. He said that I'd had such a ball on the band that he wanted me to do the next tour with him. André told him that I was singing at Mister Kelly's in Chicago. He seemed quite surprised.

• *13* •

Interim

I discovered there was life after Benny Goodman. I had a call from Oscar Marienthal who owned Mister Kelly's in Chicago. He booked me into the club for a month. It was a great club but a lousy booking, as I worked opposite harmonica player Larry Adler. He did have one of my favorite pianists with him, Ellis Larkins. As you can imagine, my fans hated Adler and his fans hated me, with the result that the club cleared out after each of our sets. It was frustrating because the Union rules allowed the house musicians to work only five nights. The club's entertainment policy was seven nights, so just as the band for the five nights got familiar with your tunes and routine, their time would be up. You would then rehearse with a new group for the additional two nights. By the time the new group was up on your tunes and routine, it was time for the five-night group. Fortunately, both groups were excellent.

One night a good singer named Lucy Reed came into the club. She had followed me in Charlie Ventura's band, so I was most anxious to impress her. The dressing rooms were upstairs, and just before my show I started down, wearing very high heels. Right behind me was the bass player. He lost his footing and fell against me, so we plummeted down the stairs together, rather like two people on a sled. We gained so much momentum that my high heels splintered when they hit the wall downstairs. The manager told me that he would postpone my show until I felt better. I decided that I'd better get on with it before I fell apart. Somehow I did a good show, and immediately following, rushed up to Lucy Reed at the bar, thinking that if she didn't like my singing I had the perfect copout! I got a standing ovation as I passed through the club toward the bar. Apparently the news of my fall was all over the club.

Once again back in Los Angeles, I got an invitation from some dear friends to join them at a little club on La Cienega Boulevard called the Excusez-Moi. One of my friends asked the owner if I could sing a tune and he agreed. As I was singing, I was distracted by a man sitting in front, laughing. I wasn't singing funny songs, so I couldn't understand what was so amusing to him. He turned out to be Cy Warner, the owner of the club. He explained that he'd been laughing because he always laughed when he liked what he heard. He offered me a job singing there on weekends, and thus began a two-year engagement that became the best singing job I have ever had.

The club was built personally by Cy and was very unusual. The customers sat on cushions on the floor around Japanese-style tables. Cy had covered the ugly high ceiling with black material, and the only light in the club came through the pinholes he had punched through the material—one over each table. Cy had removed the legs from the grand piano and set it on the floor. He dug a hole in the floor for the piano pedals and the feet of the piano player. A new sounding board was built over the piano, around the edge of which Cy built a shelf for drinks. There were cushions for customers to sit on around the piano. Above the piano on either side and attached to the wall were two seats for the singers. As I sat on my seat, my feet just touched the edge of the top of the piano which had been protectively carpeted. This placed your feet on a level with the pianist's head but right beside him. (Maybe you had to be there?!)

Newcomers were surprised and delighted when they came into the room. Cy was a singer as well, and he and I sat on the seats and alternated songs. The acoustics of the club were so superb that we didn't need a microphone. I am a quiet singer at my loudest, yet when I sang softly, every note could be heard.

Bobby Troup worked across the street at a club called the Encore. He sometimes came in between his own sets, and many of our customers would tell us that they had just come from the Encore where they heard Bobby raving about the girl singer at the Excusez-Moi, so they had come in to check me out. One of the nights when I went in to hear Bobby, he introduced me and harangued the customers for some time about going over to hear me. Finally the owner came up and told him to cool it.

After a year, Cy decided to change the policy of the club. He hired three singers in addition to the two of us. They were a girl who sang French songs and a female singing duo. It was hilarious to see the different customs we singers had all adopted before our shows. Cy took tea with lemon and honey; one girl had Seven-Up, the other

Coke; the French singer took brandy; and I had straight water, no ice. I'm sure we all felt that without these warmup techniques we'd never make it.

It's been much more than seven years and the statute of limitations has run out, so I won't jeopardize Cy's tax position if I talk about how he paid me. If it was cash, it was always under the table. Often I took goods of some sort. Once it was a half-dozen Captain's chairs. I was in Jax, my favorite clothing store one day and saw a beautiful Bonnie Cashin black leather three-quarter length jacket. I came to work raving about it. Cy's wife also had an account at Jax, so Cy told me to buy the jacket and charge it to him, and I could work it off singing in the club. When I tried to explain to Jack, the store's owner, why I was charging the coat to Cy, he looked very wise and said, "Whatever you say, dear." I knew he was thinking that Cy and I were more than boss and employee, and the more I tried to explain the situation, the wiser the owner looked. I finally gave up.

From time to time I would leave the Excusez-Moi to work at the Hungry i in San Francisco. The sound man at the Hungry i had an interesting background. He was one of the Hollywood "Unfriendly Ten," the screenwriters who refused to name names during the McCarthy era. After he did his time in prison, he was so disillusioned that he quit writing altogether for years and hid himself backstage, where he announced the acts and operated the sound system. He did a very impressive job.

The verse to "Hooray for Love" begins with the lyrics: "Here's to my best romance, here's to my worst romance, here's to my first romance, ages ago." It was my custom to point to the bass player as "best," then the piano player as "worst," alternating their roles nightly. One night, as I sang the first two phrases, I looked into the audience and, after a lapse of about eighteen years, once again gazed into the eyes of the man who had deflowered me. Here sat the original cast member of the line "here's to my first romance." I was so overcome with laughter that I not only couldn't sing the line, I couldn't even finish the song. There was no way I could explain my behavior to the audience.

The Jazz Workshop on Broadway in San Francisco was a hot jazz club in those days, and the top jazz groups in the country appeared there. One week King Pleasure was singing in the club, so on one of my intermissions at the Hungry i, I went up to hear him. James Moody, the great alto sax player, had played a wonderful chorus on "I'm in the Mood for Love," and King Pleasure had written lyrics to Moody's solo and called it "Moody's Mood for Love." Blossom Dearie sang the bridge on the original recording. Someone must have told King Pleasure that I was in the audience because when he introduced the song he asked me if I knew the bridge. I did and it was great fun to sing it with him. From then on, every time I came into the club he'd call the tune and I'd jump on the bandstand. One very busy Saturday night I was a little late getting there and he was into the second eight bars. There was no way for me to get through the throng and make it to the mike in time to sing the bridge. Involuntarily, I began to sing the bridge as I fought my way through the crowd. It was a bit like an old Bing Crosby movie.

An agent called me one day and said that one of the radio stations would play my record if I'd come down and record some station breaks and read numbers so that when put together I would be telling the listeners the time. It sounded wonderful. It's not so difficult to make a recording. The problem is getting it played, so this seemed ideal. I had made three albums to date, with André arranging and playing on all of them. The DJ hadn't done his homework because on the air he asked me how I managed to get André to arrange and play for me. I could hardly believe the question! I think I said, "He was my husband, but I like to think that he admired my singing as well." The DJ was so flabbergasted that he couldn't speak. I felt kind of sorry for him.

Upon my return to Los Angeles I sang at Ye Little Club in Beverly Hills. Every night a good-looking gent sat at the front table, listening attentively. The night I closed, he asked me if he could accompany me across the street to hear Matt Dennis. Before the evening ended he got very drunk, so I insisted on following him home. A good-looking gent who is an avid fan is difficult to resist, so I didn't. We began seeing each other. It was apparent that he had a drinking problem, but I was arrogant enough to think that I could straighten him right out. One day at the beach we were discussing our stormy relationship, and I said I thought we had two choices: either stop seeing each other altogether or get married. I was amazed when he chose the latter. I had told him the story of my unhappy breakup with André and how wary I was about making another mistake, so if he really loved me he'd withdraw the marriage proposal if he felt in his heart that he couldn't stop his excessive drinking. He won me over completely by telling me that before we met he'd never had any reason to stop drinking, but with his lovely ready-made family he had three terrific reasons. We left for rings and Vegas that same day.

Our married life was complex. I had a home and children; he had a home and a cat. I had a housekeeper who looked after the children, so we took turns sleeping at each other's house. We decided to sell his house, rent mine, and buy a larger house. During this process his drinking escalated, and we began to have arguments that bewildered me. I never quite knew what they were about. One evening my daughters ran into the house, having heard his loud voice. One look at their worried faces convinced me that I couldn't put them through any more scenes, so I asked him to move out.

The marriage lasted only twenty-eight days and had serious financial consequences for me. The child support from André would continue, but the alimony had ceased upon my remarriage. My new husband had taken over the financial burden of the house, but with his departure, my income dropped by two thirds and I was left with only child support payments. I lay in bed for a full day and cried. The next day Cy Warner happened to drop by and, hearing my sad news, offered me a job as part-time secretary in his new enterprise. The project was to build a theater-in-the-round on a large property he and his two partners owned in the Valley. The theater was to be called Valley Music Theater. Cy and the partners had set up an office and were selling stock in the company. Although it was only a part-time job, it kept me out of the poorhouse.

The mechanics of getting my children to my mother's house and from there to work in the eight months I worked for Cy were exhausting. I lived in Beverly Hills and every morning I drove my children to my mother's house in Los Angeles; from there I drove about twenty-five miles to the office in Tarzana, worked four hours, drove back to my mother's house to pick up the girls, and, finally, home.

Shelly Manne provided a bright spot in my hectic life. He had been one of the first musicians I met when I went to New York in the early 1940s. I often reminded him of how many years we'd known each other. As the years passed he learned to hate this. It's difficult to keep your age secret when someone is always mentioning how long they've known you!

Through the years Shelly complained about the clubs we all worked in. He dreamed of someday owning his own club where he would be able to run it his own way and have the kind of musical freedom he had always wanted. Some time later he opened Shelly's Manne Hole on Cahuenga in Hollywood. He was using a spectacular group: Russ Freeman on piano, Monty Budwig on bass, Conte Candoli on trumpet, Richie Kamuca on tenor sax and, of course, Shelly on drums.

Shelly offered me a job singing at the club. He apologized for the low salary—I think it was sixty dollars for the three nights. I was so thrilled to be working there I'd have done it for nothing. Later he raised my salary to seventy-five dollars, and that raise meant everything to me.

One evening I was singing "Lazy Afternoon," which I did using only piano and bass. Suddenly I heard a little light giggling from the audience. When I looked around, Shelly was making what he thought were appropriate sounds on his drums with a half dollar.

I don't know how it became a tradition, or how I heard of it, or, indeed, if it ever was, but on Sunday nights I always wore a street dress rather than a gown. One Sunday night I was sitting in the band room in my short dress and Joe Maini came in. (I had worked with Joe on Alvino Rey's band; he was a terrific alto sax player.) He took a look at my legs and said, "Thank God, you have nice legs. I've never seen you in anything but long dresses, and I thought you wore them because your legs were deformed."

My day job with its grueling travel time began to pall, despite the fun I had working on the weekend in Shelly's club. I began to think of taking a year's sabbatical in Europe in the hope of finding work as a singer. I had always longed to go to Paris, but being unable to speak French, I soon realized how impractical that was. How could I explain to a group of French-speaking musicians what I wanted in the way of accompaniment? *Comment dites-on* "a chorus and a half of Lush Life in B-flat and watch out for the tag"—?

I wrote to a musician I knew who lived in London, asking what my chances were of finding singing jobs there. I figured the language wouldn't be a factor, and perhaps after I'd been there a few months, someone might suggest a club in Paris where the musicians spoke a little English. My friend wrote back saying that the chances of working there were wonderful. He said that Cleo Laine was the best singer in London at the time. No one knew just how wonderful she was in those days, including me. We do now.

I knew if I moved to London I would have three large problems. The girls' schooling was the most important issue. They attended

Highland Hall, a private school in the San Fernando Valley, one of the Waldorf schools which has branches all over the world. The divorce settlement had included André's paying for the girls' schooling so that wasn't a problem.

I learned that there was a Waldorf school outside London, so I wrote them about the possibility of enrolling the girls for a year. Their policy was not to take students for just one year, but as my girls were already Waldorf students, they'd make an exception. The next problem was to secure a second mortgage on my house so I could finance the trip. The third was to rent my house to a responsible person for the year. Four days before my departure date I still didn't know if all my problems would be resolved, but suddenly everything fell into place and off we went as planned.

The Pan Am public relations office was right on the ball, because when we appeared at the airport the photographers were there. I insisted that the girls be the only ones in the photo since I had been divorced from André for some time. Apparently this news had escaped the PR people at Pan Am, and I didn't feel right about masquerading as someone I no longer was.

We flew first to Copenhagen for a few days so the girls could visit Tivoli Gardens, and when we arrived at the airport we were met by a Pan Am car that took us to the hotel. They told me that when we were ready to fly to London I should notify them and they'd be delighted to take us to the airport.

We had three great days in Copenhagen, but when I called Pan Am, they seemed to have misplaced my credentials, so we took a taxi. At the airport, the Pan Am lady who checked us in was downright rude, complaining about the amount of carry-on luggage we had and threatening to keep us from boarding if we didn't get rid of some of it. After a considerable hassle which included my telling her we'd flown on Pan Am from California with the same amount of luggage and had no complaints, she finally allowed us to board. I knew fame was fleeting, but four days?

• 14 •

London

I left for London in July 1963. A couple of weeks before I departed, I was in my favorite dress shop and idly mentioned to the owner that I was going to London for a year. She asked me where I'd be staying. This had been a sore subject for my mother. She was uneasy at the prospect of my traveling to London with the two girls, who were seven and nine, without having made advance hotel or flat arrangements. When I told the dress shop owner of my mother's fears, she said she had a married friend who, with her husband, had leased a mews flat in Chelsea for a year. However, the husband had come back to the States and if her friend followed him, she was obligated to pay the full year's lease whether she stayed there or not. If I could sublet this flat, it would be a Godsend to her friend. It seemed an ideal situation for me until I heard how much it would cost. When I told my mother there was a flat in London but it was too expensive for me, she insisted on paying the difference between what I had planned to pay and what the flat would cost. It was worth it to her to know my address in advance, and she was grateful that we had somewhere to go when we landed.

Our plane was late, so the estate agent I was to meet at the flat in Chelsea had gone home by the time we arrived there. The cab driver we drew at the airport was a wonderfully cheerful and helpful cockney gent. He apologized for the high fare into London, but I was only too happy to pay it, particularly when we found out that no one was at the flat to let us in. He drove us to a pay phone where he contacted the agent who came over with the key. The driver carried our heavy bags to the upstairs bedrooms and said, if I needed any assistance, I was to call him. However, if a woman answered, I was to hang up!

It was then about eight o'clock in the evening and there was no food in the flat and no market open at that hour, so we looked out our front door and spied a small restaurant about two blocks down. We set out for it, and when we came in the front door the maître d' said, "Good evening, Madam, I expect you'll want a martini and two Coca-Colas." We wanted nothing of the kind, and I was disappointed that it was so apparent that we were Americans.

I had been fortunate while living in Beverly Hills to have become friends with Pamela and James Mason. I was introduced to them by the announcer on Pamela's radio show who, by the way, was my husband of twenty-eight days. Pamela had given me the names of some of her friends and relatives and asked me to call them when I arrived. She had also told me not to bother taking slacks as they weren't being worn to any great degree at that time in London. This was 1963. The next morning, chic or not, I donned my one pair of slacks and went to the market. I didn't know then that Chelsea was an "in" place to live, nor did I know how important a "correct" address was. That morning I saw dozens of ladies wearing slacks. I had no idea that the King's Road was trendy. I lived one short block off King's Road on Elystan Place, very near Sloane Square.

After marketing, the girls and I hailed a cab and drove to the estate agent's office to pay the first month's rent. When we arrived, I pulled out all of my English money and asked the cab driver to take what he needed, plus tip. He refused, saying that it wouldn't be fair to take advantage, and when I learned what those baffling pieces of paper and metal meant, I could begin to tip. Two days in London and two wonderful cab drivers. It augured well.

The owners of the flat we sublet were in India, but left behind a perfectly marvelous cleaning lady. She and I still exchange Christmas notes. I was discussing World War II with her one day when she calmly related the most horrifying story of the bomb that had destroyed everything she owned.

I had one very bad moment when I took my check to the bank to open an account. They told me it would be a month before it could be cleared from the States. By then, of course, we'd all be on the dole. The cashier said that if I'd pay for it she'd send a telegram and the check could be cleared in a week. Although I okayed it, this did not comfort me as I was down to my last couple of pounds. Luckily a friend I had met through Pamela rang up and, in tears, I told him what had happened. Shortly after, my cleaning lady answered the door and this nice gentleman handed her an envelope containing fifty pounds, with strict instructions that I was not to think of paying it back.

One day I was returning from the market, wearing my regulation Chelsea costume—black leather trousers, black leather boots, black cashmere turtleneck sweater, and black leather jacket. As I crossed the King's Road, I saw a magnificent chauffeur-driven Rolls Royce weaving its way through traffic. In the back seat sat an elegant gentleman, his lap covered by a fur rug. As the car passed, I saw that the occupant was James Mason. I rushed out into the street, pounded on the window, and shouted his name. He immediately opened the door, greeted me, and asked me to jump in and he'd drop me home. I said I lived only a block away and it wouldn't be necessary. He then looked me up and down a few times and remarked in that wonderful English accent, "Well, my dear, you look ... delightfully ... ah ... local."

I had decided that the girls should be weekly boarders at their school, which was thirty miles out of London. They would come home on the weekend. Every Monday morning we'd take a cab to the station where they'd board the bus for Kings Langley. Once there they had a half-mile walk almost straight up the hill to the school, each carrying her school bookbag and a small suitcase containing clean clothes. We left the flat before dawn, nearly always in the pouring rain, hoping to find a cab that could get us to the bus station before the bus left. It was difficult to maintain a sense of humor.

I was given a long list of the clothing requirements at school and went to Peter Jones in Sloane Square to fulfill them. Four items on the list were unfamiliar to me: Wellingtons, plimsolls, knickers, and Liberty blouses. I was reasonably certain that Wellingtons were some sort of garter belt, so we went directly to children's lingerie. When the clerk directed me to the shoe department, I thought she must have misunderstood me. After I learned that Wellingtons were rain boots, I asked the clerk in that department where I would find plimsolls. "Right here, Madam. I believe you call them tennis shoes." Knickers were panties made from grey sweatsuit material, and the Liberty bodice turned out to be a fleecy garment worn under their short-sleeved T-shirts. They wore knickers and a garter belt which was attached to long woolen stockings. Over this were a challis long-sleeved shirt, a vest, a short pleated skirt, and the school blazer. The constant rain left the grounds soggy, so they had sturdy shoes for the outdoors and an additional pair for indoors, cleverly called "indoor shoes." These were round-toed sandals with teardrop perforations across the toes. The girls simply loathed them. (Much later they became quite fashionable among the young folks in this country.) They wore berets and heavy raincoats with button-in linings and mittens or gloves. Every weekend they brought their laundry home, and I grew weary of washing and ironing the same few pieces of clothing.

The friend I had contacted about coming to London had told Ronnie Scott and Pete King about me. Ronnie Scott and Pete King owned a jazz club which they called Ronnie Scott's. Pete King managed the club and Ronnie played there frequently. It was several months before I gained the courage to go to the club and introduce myself. Ronnie's was then on Gerard Street in a basement. I felt sure that if I walked in alone everyone would stare at me and I was too unsure of myself to allow that to happen. Eventually, in desperation, I did go down alone, and when I introduced myself, Ronnie and Pete said they'd been expecting me for weeks. I never did audition for Ronnie, but he invited me to sing on a radio show with him, after which he hired me for the club.

Engagements in Ronnie's club were for a week. I believe I was the first girl singer they ever used in the club. On opening night, after my first tune, I looked out at that British audience and had such an overwhelming sense of how far I'd come from Hamburg, Iowa, that I said, "I'm from the Midwest," and began laughing. One of my reviewers was baffled in print by what seemed a non sequitur, but it made complete sense to me.

As far as the musicians were concerned, they were identical to the ones at home—only their accents were different—so I felt at home immediately. Ronnie Scott is a very funny man; my family still uses many of his lines. For instance, when the phone rang, Ronnie always said, "Answer that, it might be the phone." And instead of "on the contrary, my dear," Ronnie always said, "on the Continent, my dear." I have been given some mighty strange looks when I deliver these lines to people who don't know me or Ronnie.

Ronnie introduced the various acts booked into the club, and I always looked forward to these introductions. One night during a Tubby Hayes quintet appearance, Ronnie announced that Tubby wouldn't be appearing that night as he'd been "taken suddenly drunk." I am a natural Ronnie Scott audience I suppose, because I laughed at the same lines every night I was there. In addition to his humor, he was a superb tenor saxophonist—pronounced "sax-*off*-on-ist" in England, with the accent on the "off." I'm still having trouble remembering how it is pronounced here.

Near the kitchen in Ronnie's old club was a small lounge area for the band and employees. There was a sink in the corner. One night, just as Ronnie announced the Tubby Hayes group, the trumpet player, Jimmy Deuchar, threw up in the sink. I was shocked and showed it. It never occurred to me that Jimmy was aware of my dismay, but the next night when he was in good shape and Ronnie was once again announcing Tubby's group, he ran over to the sink and made retching sounds, then looked over at me and chuckled.

In 1963 a good American singer was a rarity in London, so I got more rave reviews than I could hope for, and every six weeks or so I worked for a week at Ronnie's. Most likely Ronnie's customers don't miss the old club on Gerard, but I have a great fondness for it. You walked downstairs to a ticket window, turned right and entered a small hall, then turned left to the bar area and straight ahead to the showroom. The office was a very small, cramped, cluttered room under the stairs, and when it rained, which was mostly, the hallway and office would get very wet. There was a black and white television set in the office, and we would stand around watching it between shows. It was so crowded we had to stand shoulder to shoulder.

Stan Tracey, the pianist I worked with, was a droll character and very witty. One night we were watching some old World War I footage with the speeded-up look those old films have. The soldiers were practically running instead of marching. Stan said, "There was none of your strolling about in those days, was there?"

I was seeing an attorney (called a solicitor there) and he was extremely jealous, for no reason. A certain amount of public relations is absolutely necessary to the entertainer. It's not as simple as singing two or three sets a night and rushing back to the dressing room between shows. The customers want to meet and mingle with you. It's a pleasure for me to sit and chat with them. My gent was so jealous that after I had sat with a party for about ten minutes he'd appear and just stand silently in front of the table until acknowledged. This put a damper on both the customers and me. I was never able to make him understand that this was part of my job. I repeatedly warned him that our relationship couldn't withstand this kind of intense supervision. He continued to follow me around the club until he destroyed all of my feelings for him.

At Christmas my parents came over for a month's visit. They happened to arrive while I was doing one of my weeks at Ronnie's. The Bennett family is a sentimental lot, bordering on maudlin, so through the years when my parents would come to hear me sing, they and I would always cry. This night my parents brought my two daughters and we all had a good cry. I explained the circumstances to the audience and introduced my family; the audience loved it.

Pete King became my manager and expanded my one-week engagement to two at the club. After the two weeks were up, I was booked on a big television show and would finally realize my dream of working a few gigs on the Continent. I made arrangements to send the girls home to America to live with my parents until I could fulfill my contracts. One week into the Ronnie gig my father called me to say that my dear mother had had a heart attack and it would be forty-eight hours before we would know if she was to live or die. My newfound British friends rallied around and made all the arrangements for me to leave the next day. I left most things behind, and my friends packed and sent everything on to me.

My mother lived for another three months so I was able to spend a great deal of time with her, doing her cleaning and cooking with joy. She and I have always been extremely close, but unable to verbalize our love in any way except that of the loving insult. One day after I had been working at her house, she put her arms around me and tried to tell me how much she appreciated all I had done for her. I quickly put an end to that by telling her to be careful, I might get the idea she loved me.

I asked my father to move in with me for a few months after my mother's death. He had had a run of deaths in a very short period of time. First, his mother, then his uncle, and now his wife. We were watching television one night quite late and the phone rang. We looked at each other fearfully. Quickly I took inventory of my remaining loved ones, assured myself that the two girls were safely asleep in the bedroom, and said, "Relax, dad, everyone's dead." In fact, I made a great many bizarre remarks for the first few months after my beloved mother's death.

It took a year to accomplish it, but I decided to move to London permanently since I had been doing so well as a singer when I left. The day I put the house on the market, the first people who saw it bought it. I'm afraid I confused the real estate agent when I said that if I'd known he was going to actually sell my house I wouldn't have put it on the market. The two girls and I still remember that house with love. I have owned two houses since then, and each is just a larger version of that little house.

One of the good things about my earlier move to London had been that my money seemed to go a lot farther there, but it was still a struggle. Pamela Mason had often heard me talking about my vanished alimony, and she seemed to feel that a good attorney could help me, so she told attorney Marvin Mitchelson my story. He was able to almost double the amount of money I received monthly for child support, the compromise being that I call half of it "alimony" and pay taxes on it. This would give André a tax break as he could write off alimony but not child support.

I had the movers come in and go over each piece of furniture. If they said it would be more to move than replace, I planned to sell or give it away. My problem was that I was an avid reader and owned over a thousand books, all of which I'd read and wanted desperately to take to England with me. The movers disabused me of that notion by telling me it would cost fifty dollars per shelf section. Since each section contained only about forty books, it was not financially feasible to transport them to England. My friends all said I should just replace the books in second-hand stores in London, but I hated the thought of having a bunch of books that I hadn't personally read, so I put all of my books into storage, along with my good pieces of furniture. I decided to "think about it tomorrow."

I flew to London two weeks in advance of my girls and managed to find a flat at Marble Arch, a very convenient address, at least for my purposes. The girls were not so fortunate. They had so hated being weekly boarders at The New School on our prior trip that they persuaded me to let them travel to and from school each day. This involved (once again in the semidarkness) walking three blocks, crossing the busy Edgeware Road, waiting for a local bus, riding in it for a mile, and transferring to the bus that took them to the foot of the aforementioned steep hill. They were on the second bus for an hour. Then, after school, they had the same trip in reverse. It was impossible for me to take a flat near their school because I worked nights and public transportation was no longer running by the time I finished working. Taking a cab from Kings Langley, where the school was located, was out of the question. It was thirty miles. The girls understood this and made the round trip daily without complaint. It took its toll on me, because every morning after I sent them off I peered out the fifth story window into the dim morning light and watched those four little legs plodding toward the Edgeware Road and the beginning of their long day.

I'm not sure I have ever appreciated all the modern conveniences at my disposal until I lived in London. Although I didn't feel particularly deprived when I lived there, our flat was five flights up and the building had no elevator. The kitchen was an idle rumor, the bathroom wintry, our dishes courtesy of Woolworth, and furniture indescribably shabby. I did rent a television set and piano. I carried the laundry to the laundromat twice a week, waited until it was washed and dried, and carried it back up five flights. The supermarket was about ten blocks away, so I bought a Raleigh folding bicycle and for about three dollars rent per month, stored it in a corner of the office of a combination gas station and monthly parking lot.

It was terrifying to cycle to the market because, when I approached the Edgeware Road and had to turn right from the left lane, I had great difficulty in keeping my composure. I was certain that any minute I would be felled by a car. The trip home from the market, loaded with bags of groceries, required even more courage.

My daughters grew up hearing, "Look to the left when you cross the street," but in England I had to retrain them to look right. This retraining went on five times, what with our two trips back and forth, and it's a wonder we weren't run down by a car. Another bit of confusion that I have been unable to clear up is the difference in the way the British and Americans designate their floors. Here the first floor is the ground floor; in England, the first floor is our second floor. I often enter the elevator here at home and have to think which button to press if I want the second floor.

A familiar sight in London was a bass player whom I never met but very often saw riding his bicycle down the street, his huge bass in a canvas sack, the strap of which he wore over his shoulder. He and I always grinned widely at each other every time we passed.

Marble Arch is right by Hyde Park corner, and there are underground tunnels from our corner to Hyde Park, making the trip simple to negotiate. The traffic is fierce at that intersection, so it was a great comfort to me to know the girls could get to the park, underground, without dodging traffic. We often heard first-rate musician/singers playing and singing in those tunnels for coins. Alicia, who for a long time lived in London, would sometimes sing and play her violin in those tunnels for money. From time to time when she was short of money, she'd play until she had enough for a nice dinner. After André moved there, she was always terrified that he might find out what she was doing.

When the Playboy Club was opened in London, I was hired to sing in one of the rooms. The dressing room for the entertainers wasn't finished, so the manager said I could use the bunnies' dressing room. I went into the toilet and found a large rubber falsie on the floor. I secreted it under my gown and went back into the dimly lit band room and asked the band if they'd like to see one of the bunnies' boobs. They said they'd be delighted, so I whipped out the falsie.

Claudia left her guitar on the bus one day, so I called the bus company and they said that the bus was just arriving in the barn. Rather than have us wait a few days until the guitar could be transferred to lost and found, we could meet the bus driver at the Hyde Park Corner stop at 8:15 p.m. and the driver would hand over the guitar. That was good news because we had spent a lot of time cooling our heels at the lost and found building, looking for the several umbrellas we had left on the bus in the past.

The day Claudia left the guitar on the bus was also the day of my opening night at the new Playboy Club, so I dropped Claudia off at the bus stop and went on to work. I felt quite secure in leaving Claudia, since she was waiting by the well-lit underground tunnel leading directly to our corner. The next day she told me that a man had come up to her as she waited and waved his penis at her. It was raining at the time, so she simply said to him, "Mister, you better put that away or it'll get wet." He was so undone by the logic of this remark that he slunk away. At that time Claudia was just eleven years old. I, however, aged considerably upon hearing her story.

Meanwhile, Ronnie Scott had opened his beautiful new club on Frith Street. It was quite a shock to me to learn that, in the year I had been home in California, several really first-rate American singers had settled in London. Although I still worked at Ronnie's from time to time, the novelty of the American singer had definitely worn off. Mark Murphy and Ernestine Anderson were now living in London, and Blossom Dearie came over from New York frequently. If one American singer fell ill, there was another one waiting in the wings.

Blossom Dearie came to our flat one day, and we had a lovely musical afternoon. She sang and played some beautiful and obscure tunes. One was particularly nice. It was called "The Shadow of Your

Smile." She told me it had been written by Johnny Mandel. A couple of weeks later André happened to be in London, and he and I took the girls to Hampton Court. I told him about this beautiful song and asked him if he'd heard it. He looked at me with a mixture of suspicion and amazement. Yes, he'd heard it; it had won the Academy Award for best song that year!

Bennie Green, a bright, articulate critic who wrote for the *Manchester Guardian* in those days, had a series of half-hour television programs saluting various songwriters. He asked me to share the program with him. We took the train to Manchester and had some great times doing these shows. The camera would open on Bennie, sitting in an impressive chair, giving a bit of the songwriters' backgrounds, then shift over to me with the rhythm section, demonstrating the songs. These shows were shown on television late at night, so we were able to get back to the hotel in time to watch them. After the first show, Bennie called me and said he hadn't had the nerve to order a television set for his room and did I have one? If so, could he watch the show with me? I hadn't had the courage either, but with Bennie there, I felt I could handle it so I ordered a set. We watched the show together and were pleased with how well it turned out. Although I am normally very vain, I have never worried about how I look when I'm appearing on television; my worry is how I sound.

After a year in London I got to thinking about my widowed father and about André, who was still living in Bel-Air at the time. I thought about how selfish I was in keeping the children away from their father and grandfather when I was doing so little singing in London. I decided to come home. Imagine my surprise when I learned that my father had remarried and André had been appointed conductor of the London Symphony. He and I waved as we passed each other in the air.

• 15 •

Mundell Lowe

I returned to Los Angeles in 1966 and bought a home in Studio City. My daughters went back to Highland Hall. I immediately called up the "Jimmy Rowles Network"—these are the friends who keep track of where he's playing so we can all go to hear him—and I learned that he was at Donte's, a club in North Hollywood. In those days it was a piano bar, but over one blindingly quick weekend, they built a bandstand and began to present larger groups and, later, big bands.

I became good friends with the owners, Sunny and Bill McKay and Carey Leverett. I felt very comfortable dropping by Donte's any night I felt bored or wanted to hear some good jazz. I sang there a couple of times, but in order to make my house payments, I began working for Edward Anhalt, an award-winning screenwriter.

I was sitting next to Max Bennett, the bass player, in Donte's one night. Although he and I are not related, we call each other Bruz and Sis. A new face appeared in the doorway. I asked Max who it belonged to, and he told me it was Mundell Lowe's. "Isn't he a black guitar player from New York?" I asked. "No, he's a white guitar player and he lives out here." I had heard of Mundell for years, always playing with the likes of Charlie Parker, Prez, and at Café Society, so I assumed he was black.

Mundell was married at the time, but occasionally I did see him in Donte's. There seemed no question that we were both fascinated with each other, but he had young children and because of the scars caused by his parent's breaking up when he was eight years old he was determined to stay at home until his youngest turned fourteen.

Jimmy Lyons and Ralph Gleason had hired me to sing at the first Monterey Jazz Festival in 1958. It was so disorganized and chaotic I didn't go back until 1970. Every year or so Leonard and Jane Feather would ask me to come with them to the festival, but I always said no. In 1970 I suddenly said yes. Imagine my surprise and delight when I opened the festival program and saw that Mundell was part of the always spectacular house band. (He later replaced John Lewis as musical director.) I guess our romance began that year, although he was still living at home. I was lucky if I saw him every two weeks. Another year or so passed before Mundell left home. I can't believe how lucky I am to have him.

Mundell wasn't aware that I was a singer, and I was fearful that, if he didn't like the way I sang, he'd never be able to say so and would probably lose interest in me. Although it is an old saw, if you look up the word "insecure" in the dictionary, you will find my picture right next to the word!

One weekend in Big Sur after much wine he picked up his guitar and I sang for him. It was a wonderful evening and we have been working together ever since. I have enormous regard for his talent, and the perk of having someone write all of your arrangements and be willing (not always!) to rehearse makes me one lucky girl singer.

Mundell and Jimmy Lyons looked so much alike that people constantly mixed them up. It led to some pretty funny episodes. When the mistake was made, both of them would pretend to be the other until the poor soul asking the question finally realized his error. They called each other "bruz" and had a very loving relationship. Jimmy and I had been friends since I met him in 1950 when I was singing in San Francisco. He had a very popular radio show and had interviewed me a few times on the air.

Mundell proposed to me in Monterey, and we immediately told Jimmy. He suggested we be married at the annual Thursday night private party that precedes the festival's opening. That year, 1975, rather than the traditional party at the fairgrounds, it was being held at Doc's Lab on Cannery Row, the actual location for John Steinbeck's book *Cannery Row*. Jimmy and my daughter Claudia Previn were our witnesses.

We stood on an outdoor platform behind the lab and said our "I do's" facing Judge Eldred (a festival board member) and the ocean. Clark Terry made all of us cry with his beautiful solo on "When I Fall in Love." Each year the regular festival crew kept track of how many years we'd been married. (Which is sometimes more than Mundell does!)

Every year our anniversary invariably fell on one of the festival days. One year it fell on the Thursday party night. Although we didn't know it, a huge cake had been provided for us, appropriately inscribed, and Clark Terry was to pop out from behind a bush and play "When I Fall in Love" as he had on our wedding night. Mundell was doing the Merv Griffin show in those days and couldn't make the party, so I started without him. In the end, Clark didn't pop out of the bushes and when I asked him why, he said he didn't want to do it unless Mundell was there too. It seems to me that he might have at least played half a chorus for me.

Perhaps this would be a good time to talk about the musical relationship between a singer and her accompanist/boyfriend or husband. I thought my situation was unique, but since then have discussed this with several other singers who are either married to or are an "item" with their accompanists and they have had identical experiences. One singer had to give up working with her boyfriend because he was so unforgiving. Another couple has no problem because she does whatever her fellow wants her to. I can't do that because I have definite ideas of what I want to sing and how I want to sing it. When I was married to André and he accompanied me, there was never any friction—at least not musically! In analyzing this, I concluded that I was very much a student of his as far as choosing material was concerned. I knew all the good Tin Pan Alley songs and none of the show tunes, so he was always in charge. I had never had such sensitive accompaniment before, so it was a great joy to sing the tunes he suggested. André told me a story about himself, Lennie Hayton, and Lena Horne. Lena had heard a wonderful Jerome Kern/Dorothy Fields tune, "Remind Me." This is a sixty-four bar tune (as opposed to the usual thirty-two), and it keeps changing. It doesn't follow the standard form, and to fake it by hearing just the melody sung is almost impossible. Lena sang it to Lennie and André, and at each change, the two men argued that she had to be wrong—the tune couldn't possibly go that way. Eventually they found a copy of it and Lena was absolutely correct. (Girl singers don't get no respect, either!)

I couldn't begin to understand why this is, but when Mundell and I first began to work together, rehearsal was a nightmare for me. He was impatient and often rude. I would begin to cry, which didn't help my "chops." Instead of comforting me he would insist that we "get on with it." I said that in all my years of singing I had never had an accompanist be rude to me and I couldn't understand why he was so unkind. Once I thought about it, I realized that my former accompanists were being paid to play for me, whereas Mundell was not, and maybe I was being unfair in expecting to be coddled. I promised that in the future I would consult him before accepting a gig. This changed the situation completely, and although occasionally he's still short with me, I can see him remind himself to be nice!

When I have a gig coming up, I begin rehearsing with Mundell at least two weeks ahead. I have always prided myself on being a consistent singer. I sing in tune, and although I don't always sing as well as I want to, it is at least fairly decent. Because I seem to have terminal frogs in my throat, rehearsals don't always go well and I frequently cry in frustration. At one point, after about ten days of rehearsing my show, I began crying and said I didn't seem to be getting any better. Mundell broke me up by saying, "Yes, you are. You didn't cry until the third tune today!"

It was a big change, going from piano accompaniment to guitar. Naturally more can be done on piano, since it is such a large instrument, than on the guitar. In fact, when my throat is troubling me, the piano can cover more easily some of the rough spots. The guitar, on the other hand, can leave you hanging out there. I am now so used to guitar accompaniment that I am a little reluctant to sit in with a piano player!

I had essentially retired from singing after my mother died. She had been the babysitter made in heaven, so after her death I simply quit thinking about singing. I was working as a secretary and trying to raise my two daughters. Mundell's son moved in with us, and I made the decision to keep working for Edward Anhalt until Mundell's son turned eighteen. His other children were married and settled.

Charlie Chiarenza, the guitarist once with the Baja Marimba Band, obviously saved his money and was able to buy Alfonse's, a club on Riverside Drive in Toluca Lake, California. He immediately set about making it a jazz room, using a different group every night except Friday and Saturday, when the chosen group worked both nights. My only singing at the time consisted of an occasional musical evening at our house or at the house of friends. I was mostly contented with this, but every time Mundell and I went into the club, Charlie asked me when I was coming to work for him. I always said no. Finally, I told him to set a date and I'd do it. This began a "sometime" career, usually at Alfonse's.

There is no question that a compliment from a peer is high praise indeed. Just before the last show one night at Alfonse's, I saw bassist Andy Simpkins come in with drummer Harold Jones, two-thirds of Sarah Vaughan's trio. I remember praying that Sarah wouldn't come in or, if she did, I wouldn't know it. A dear friend of mine knew Sarah and sat with her during my show. As it ended, Sarah said to my friend, "The kid sings good." In view of the fact that I am a couple of years older than Sarah, I had trouble deciding which compliment I liked better, "kid" or "good"!

One year the owner of The Bull's Head, a pub in Barnes, England, booked Mundell. He also booked other gigs all over England for whatever American jazz musician was currently playing at his pub. After a couple of years I was booked into some of the same clubs, and Mundell and I did a few BBC radio broadcasts. This led to bookings in Scotland, Ireland, and Wales.

Mundell and I moved to San Diego in 1989 and immediately hooked up with a wonderful flute player called Holly Hofmann. She has become our surrogate daughter and employer! She booked the Palace Bar at the Horton Grande for a few years, and both Mundell and I worked there for her. The last gig I did there came about when I complained to her that I wanted to announce my retirement but I couldn't get a gig. After she stopped laughing, she gave me a night, but I had such a good time I'm still singing whenever somebody rings the phone!

• 16 •

Summing Up

There's no question that I'm an unreconstructed band chick. If I hadn't been sitting on the bandstand all those years, you can be sure I would have been standing in front of it. I am delighted to be a part of the musical community. It's an exclusive club, and unless you're a player you will have a difficult time joining it. Even then, your musical opinions will probably not be wholly accepted: the compliment paid a musician by one of his or her peers means more than the same compliment from a nonmusician. Yes, there is a sort of snobbery among musicians. It's certainly not that we don't want praise from the audience when it's warranted; it's just that when an associate pays a compliment it must mean that you're doing something right.

Thank God for the many discerning fans, some of whom are frustrated musicians and singers and most of whom know exactly what they're hearing. There's nothing more disheartening to me when singing in a club, and for some reason having trouble with my voice, than to have someone in the audience tell me how wonderful I sound. It's no comfort to know that, as far as the public is concerned, you "got away with it" and the audience didn't know you were having difficulties. I find it almost impossible to shake off my depression when I have had a bad night. I can actually remember notes I sang years ago that were a little off!

I have dedicated this book to my mother, who insisted that I learn to play the piano. Although I no longer play, when I need to know a new song, I am able to fake my way through the piano part well enough to learn it. I have conducted a few clinics, and one of the things I stress is the importance of being able to read music. No person sets out to become, say, a doctor and immediately puts up a shingle—he or she faces years of schooling before becoming a doctor. It seems to follow that, if you plan to make singing your profession, you need to acquire the necessary skills. By way of explanation, I heard that a society band in New York was looking for a girl singer. This was the last job I wanted, but I needed the money. I was hired temporarily because I could read and was able to join the band with little or no rehearsal. I stayed on with them until they could find a girl singer who didn't mind singing with a band that used a tenor saxophone on lead. To get an idea of the difference between alto playing lead and tenor playing lead, listen to a society band. They all use tenor on lead. No self-respecting jazz band would use anything but alto on lead. When I sang with Benny Goodman, I used a little notebook in which I laid out the routine of each tune I sang: how many bars in the introduction, how many choruses, and if there was a tag. I still have a little notebook—these days it contains the names of the songs I know and in what key I sing them, categorized as "Up Tunes" and "Ballads."

There is no question that there are marvelous singers around who cannot read a note and are not handicapped in the least by this. They are obviously blessed with very good ears. The advantage to being able to read music is that you have options nonreaders do not have. There are hundreds of singers in Chicago, New York, and Los Angeles who may sing well enough to be soloists but haven't gotten a break. However, since they are schooled musicians with excellent reading skills, they can make a very handsome living singing in vocal groups. During the fifties I did a lot of choir work at MGM, where it was essential to be able to read. There is also a lot of jingle work and a high demand for back-up singers.

When I was in high school, I sang in the Baptist choir. Since then, I have sung in choirs in various churches. It is an invaluable way to hone your skills. Of course, some of the choir singers do not read very well, and some, not at all. The director is grateful for every additional choir member and is more than willing to help you learn your part. Also, it won't hurt you to be in church on Sunday!

When I was with Alvino Rey, we would play medleys of tunes for dancing. He insisted that I hold up my fingers to indicate in what key I would be singing my tune in the medley. Holding up one finger is one flat, or F; two fingers is two flats or B flat; three fingers is three flats, or E flat; four fingers, four flats, or A flat, etc. The fingers are held down for the flat keys and up for the sharp keys. It was wonderful training.

Rocky Coluccio, a.k.a. Cole, gave me some valuable advice when we were on Alvino's band in 1947. I was inclined to fall in love with certain notes in a song and hold them too long. Meanwhile, the harmony behind me had changed, producing a dissonant sound. Rocky made me painfully aware of this and I haven't made that mistake since. Be aware that when the harmony changes you need to do the same. In fact, if you listen carefully to many of the singers today, you will hear that they need to heed Rocky's advice.

There are occasions when the pianist hired by the club may barely be able to read your music. That creates a big problem for me because I don't do a lot of familiar tunes. A pianist's attempt to fake my music is dispiriting to me, to say the least, but I've learned to rise above these distractions because the audience deserves your very best. When the pianist is good, however, life is wonderful. Back in the forties when Milt Page was my pianist, he would often say before the show, "Sing it good, baby." (Not grammatical, but accurately quoted.) I would tell him that if he played it good I'd sing it good. It's a great feeling when the singer and accompanist "feed" each other. It's a lot like having a fascinating conversation with a friend. So many nights are more or less routine, but occasionally you and the group will be inspired. There's no high like it.

While trying to analyze why girl singers have been given such a bad rap, I've discussed this with a couple of girl singers. We agree that in the old days singers couldn't read music and knew little or nothing about harmony, so the musicians felt they hadn't paid their dues. Singers get more attention and applause than the hard-working cats in the band and often are paid more money, which also causes resentment.

I was lucky enough to have studied voice in high school, and although I was aiming to be a soprano and am now a jazz singer, I have found my early classical training to be invaluable. Proper breathing through the diaphragm is vital if you are to carry long phrases. The shoulders should never move: that is an unmistakable sign of improper breathing. When singing a ballad, or indeed an up tune, you should be able to carry over the lyricist's thought without breathing in the middle of a phrase. Some renowned singers are guilty of splitting words during a long phrase. For instance, during the song "Embraceable You," it would be unforgivable to break "embraceable" into "embray-(breath)-ceable you," demonstrating the importance of breath control—knowing where to breathe so the words flow—and are not chopped up, thereby defeating the purpose of the lyricist.

I have always preferred songs with a wide range and particularly like it when the song does a lot of skipping from high to low.

This necessitates tremendous control and an impeccable ear, which brings up another of the "musts" for a singer: the ability to sing in tune. Keeping time and singing in tune are basic requirements. Don't leave home without them.

Today, with the explosion of schools for jazz, covering every possible aspect of music, girl singers have become musicians in their own right. They are terrific readers, know about harmonics, and are no longer dismissed as mere window dressing. When I was coming up, there was no such thing as a jazz workshop or school. My workshop was on the road with the band. I discarded and kept many routines as I sang my tunes nightly.

It takes a terrific ear to be able to improvise! Unless you can improve the melody or sing something as well as it is written, it's best to stick to the melody. Jazz singing cannot be taught. The best a singer can do if she doesn't have the ear is to hire an arranger to write the improvisation for her. A good arranger can make a big difference. The great pianist Jimmy Rowles made it a point to know the lyrics to every tune a singer sang when he accompanied her, and it enabled him to support her when she needed it. I have worked with accompanists who were so busy playing runs and flowery phrases behind my solo that I got totally distracted. One night, I simply stopped singing, flung my hand in the pianist's direction and said, "Take it!" (No wonder jazz critic Ralph Gleason told me I had a reputation for being death on pianists!)

Another thing that cannot be taught is the ability to keep time. One afternoon I ran into Irv Cotler on a break from a television show featuring a famous male singer. (Irv Cotler was Frank Sinatra's drummer for many years.) Irv was out in the parking lot behind the station complaining bitterly about his job: in addition to playing drums, it was his task to stand under the camera and in front of the singer, conducting him, to keep him from getting too far off the beat. Most singers sing with good time, but to swing requires more than just keeping time. Frank Sinatra, Sarah Vaughan, Ella Fitzgerald, and Carmen McRae were swinging singers; in fact, they could make ballads swing. Of course, both Carmen and Sarah played piano, which certainly gave them the advantage of knowing what fit harmonically. I have no explanation for why some singers can swing and others cannot, unless perhaps listening, playing, and singing jazz all your life make it second nature.

If you have a regular gig, it is easy to keep your voice in shape. If not, it is important to do a little warming up each day, even if it is simply singing some of the songs from your repertoire. When I am working, I run through all the songs I will be singing, daily, without accompaniment. It's enough to not only warm up my voice, but it also enables me to remember all the lyrics and arrangements.

Recording has changed dramatically since I made my first record. Then the singer stood in the studio with the musicians, a sort of folding glass screen around her. Today the singer is often in another room entirely, with glass on the side facing the musicians, wearing headphones. We never wore headphones in the old days. You've probably seen announcers or singers with one hand cupped over an ear in order to hear themselves better—that drove me crazy. The first time I wore headphones it frightened me. Once you're used to it, it is clear how far superior it is to the old way.

I have always taken great pride in recording a song in one, at most two, takes. This is no longer necessary. The engineers can patch in one note, a phrase, an ending—whatever the problem is, they can fix it.

During a low period of my life when I was pregnant, separated from my musician-husband, and in therapy, the psychologist suggested that I break out of my pattern of dating only musicians and try dating men in other professions. For about five years I changed my pattern, but although I dated some wonderful business types, something was missing for me. There's really nothing like being in the company of a fellow musician, listening to someone play a familiar song and suddenly hear an unexpectedly delightful change of harmony. It's a great feeling to look at your companion and see that he is as pleased as you are with the new direction this familiar tune has taken. No need to explain. You know that you both know.

Years ago I was living in a rooming house with eight other women. (We were called "girls" in those days!) We wandered in and out of each other's rooms. One evening I was telling them how important music is, how enriching, how drab life would be without it. Imagine my surprise when one of the women told me that she and her boyfriend neither knew nor cared about music and their lives together were as fulfilling and satisfying as mine. It had never occurred to me in my great arrogance that untold numbers of people were getting along famously without music. Well, I am getting along famously but I have music too!

Rumors have been flying for years that big bands are coming back. Nothing would make me happier, but if they did, where would they play? Most of the great (and dreadful) ballrooms we played in across the country no longer present big bands. Indeed, I wonder if they still exist, and if they do, what do they present there? Elitch Gardens in Denver; Frank Dailey's Meadowbrook in New Jersey; Steel Pier, Atlantic City; the Trianon Ballroom, Chicago; Deshler-Wallich Hotel, Columbus, Ohio; Casa Mañana, Aragon Ballroom, and the Casino Gardens in Los Angeles—these last three are gone.

Aside from Maynard Ferguson and Les Brown, no band with its original leader comes to mind. The rest of the bands traveling around are being fronted by a former sideman, their leaders having been "kicked upstairs." The bands of Glenn Miller, Jimmy Dorsey, Count Basie, Tommy Dorsey, Harry James, and Duke Ellington all fall into this latter category.

As far back as I can remember, there have been so-called "rehearsal" bands in Los Angeles and New York City. Musicians get together and rehearse from time to time, occasionally performing one or two nights in a local club. Often the band members are much the same; only the book and the leader change. It's not uncommon to see the leader from one night playing in a band the next night for a leader who was *his* sideman the night before.

Los Angeles has some really great local bands. There are Bill Berry, The Frank Capp Juggernaut, Bob Florence, Roger Neumann, Louis Bellson, and Bill Holman. Most of the bands use certain key players who best reflect the band's sound, but the rest of the band is interchangeable. All the bands are organized and serious. The problem is that the sidemen are predominantly studio musicians who make a comfortable living and can't afford to go out on the road for the salaries being paid today. No band leader could pay the money they can make in the studios.

Canada has the sensational Rob McConnell band. The sidemen certainly don't live on the income derived from playing with the band; its members also make their basic living recording and doing studio calls.

I'm fairly sure that June Christy was the last band singer to "make it" doing a single act after she left Stan Kenton. I understand that Basie's band has a girl singer, but I doubt that it will start a trend. Occasionally Bill Berry adds a girl singer. Frank Capp uses Ernie Andrews, but more as an added attraction than as the "boy singer."

My personal favorite band singers were Maryanne McCall with Woody's band, Peggy Lee with Benny Goodman, Helen Forrest when she was with Harry James, and Doris Day on Les Brown's band. There are many fine singers who have never known the joy of singing with a good big band. I miss it every time I hear a swinging big band.

Fortunately, many colleges have jazz band programs, and they turn out some formidable players. Berklee and North Texas State University have been supplying bands with musicians for years. Buddy Rich's and Woody Herman's bands were filled with graduates from one or the other school. Colleges also provide concert halls in which to present the few remaining working bands. Hearing a band in concert, free from smoke, noise, and drunks is rewarding, but I really miss the excitement generated in a ballroom, from the fans standing in front digging the band, to the dancers out on the floor.

I'm sorry Charlie Barnet joined "the big band in the sky" because if he were still around I'd ask for my old job back!

Index